D1467418

The Importance of

The Importance of Germ Theory

Toney Allman

ReferencePoint
Press®

San Diego, CA

ReferencePoint
Press®

About the Author

Toney Allman holds degrees from Ohio State University and the University of Hawaii. She currently lives in Virginia, where she enjoys a rural lifestyle as well as researching and writing about a variety of topics for students.

© 2016 ReferencePoint Press, Inc.
Printed in the United States

For more information, contact:
ReferencePoint Press, Inc.
PO Box 27779
San Diego, CA 92198
www. ReferencePointPress.com

LIBRARY OF CONGRESS CATALOGING-IN-PUBLICATION DATA

Allman, Toney.
  The importance of germ theory / by Toney Allman.
    pages cm. -- (Importance of scientific theory series)
  Audience: Grades 9 to 12.
  Includes bibliographical references and index.
  ISBN-13: 978-1-60152-890-2 (hardback)
  ISBN-10: 1-60152-890-6 (hardback)
  1. Germ theory of disease--Juvenile literature. 2. Diseases--Causes and theories of causation--Juvenile literature. I. Title.
  RB151.A45 2016
  616--dc23
                                                                    2014047685

CONTENTS

FOREWORD

What is the nature of science? The authors of "Understanding the Scientific Enterprise: The Nature of Science in the Next Generation Science Standards," answer that question this way: "Science is a way of explaining the natural world. In common parlance, science is both a set of practices and the historical accumulation of knowledge. An essential part of science education is learning science and engineering practices and developing knowledge of the concepts that are foundational to science disciplines. Further, students should develop an understanding of the enterprise of science as a whole—the wondering, investigating, questioning, data collecting and analyzing."

Examples from history offer a valuable way to explore the nature of science and understand the core ideas and concepts around which all life revolves. When English chemist John Dalton formulated a theory in 1803 that all matter consists of small, indivisible particles called atoms and that atoms of different elements have different properties, he was building on the ideas of earlier scientists as well as relying on his own experimentation, observation, and analysis. His atomic theory, which also proposed that atoms cannot be created or destroyed, was not entirely accurate, yet his ideas are remarkably close to the modern understanding of atoms. Intrigued by his findings, other scientists continued to test and build on Dalton's ideas until eventually—a century later—actual proof of the atom's existence emerged.

The story of these discoveries and what grew from them is presented in *The Importance of Atomic Theory*, one volume in Reference-Point's series *The Importance of Scientific Theory*. The series strives to help students develop a broader and deeper understanding of the nature of science by examining notable ideas and events in the history of science. Books in the series focus on the development and outcomes of atomic theory, cell theory, germ theory, evolution theory, plate tectonic theory, and more. All books clearly state the core idea and explore changes in thinking over time, methods of experimentation and observation, and societal impacts of these momentous theories and discoveries. Each volume includes a visual chronology; brief descriptions of important people; sidebars that highlight and further explain key events and concepts; "words in context" vocabulary; and, where possible, the words of the scientists themselves.

Through richly detailed examples from history and clear discussion of scientific ideas and methods, *The Importance of Scientific Theory* series furthers an appreciation for the essence of science and the men and women who devote their lives to it. As the authors of "Understanding the Scientific Enterprise: The Nature of Science in the Next Generation Science Standards" write, "With the addition of historical examples, the nature of scientific explanations assumes a human face and is recognized as an ever-changing enterprise."

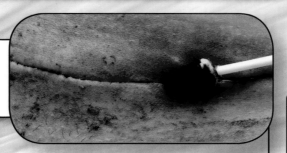

1865
Joseph Lister begins using antiseptics to prevent wound infections after surgery.

1876
Robert Koch provides the first proof of the germ theory of disease with his investigation of anthrax bacteria.

1796
Edward Jenner develops the first vaccine, which protects against smallpox.

1850
Ignaz Semmelweis advocates hand washing by physicians to prevent puerperal, or childbed, fever, but his work is largely ignored.

1710 / 1810   1830   1850   1870

1674
Antonie van Leeuwenhoek refines the microscope and becomes the first person to view living microorganisms.

1854
A cholera epidemic in London ends after physician John Snow removes a water pump handle to prevent people from drawing water from the contaminated well.

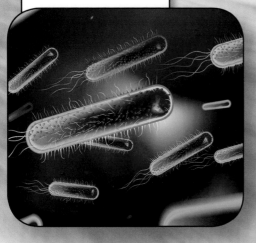

1862
Louis Pasteur develops the germ theory of disease.

1877
Robert Koch publishes his scientific criteria, known as Koch's postulates, for demonstrating experimentally that specific microorganisms cause specific diseases.

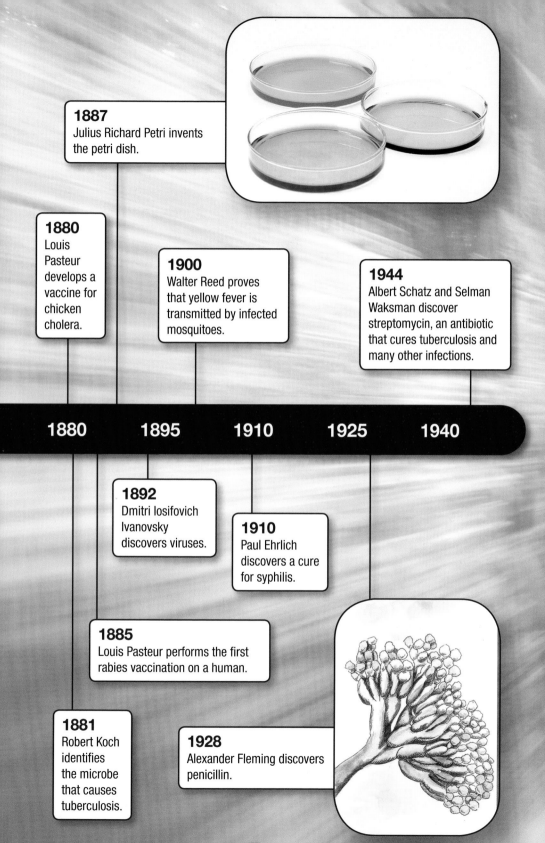

1887
Julius Richard Petri invents the petri dish.

1880
Louis Pasteur develops a vaccine for chicken cholera.

1900
Walter Reed proves that yellow fever is transmitted by infected mosquitoes.

1944
Albert Schatz and Selman Waksman discover streptomycin, an antibiotic that cures tuberculosis and many other infections.

1880   1895   1910   1925   1940

1892
Dmitri Iosifovich Ivanovsky discovers viruses.

1910
Paul Ehrlich discovers a cure for syphilis.

1885
Louis Pasteur performs the first rabies vaccination on a human.

1881
Robert Koch identifies the microbe that causes tuberculosis.

1928
Alexander Fleming discovers penicillin.

INTRODUCTION

Transforming Medicine and the World

THE CORE IDEA

Germ theory states that many diseases are caused by the presence and actions of microscopic living organisms that invade the bodies of people and other living things. "Germ" is an old English word meaning "seed" or "sprout," but in the medical sense it refers to any microbe or microorganism that causes disease—whether it is a bacterium, a virus, a fungus, or a protozoan. Germ theory encompasses four critical elements. It says that the agents of some diseases are microbes or germs; that these diseases are communicable and can pass from one person to another, either directly or indirectly; that the disease-causing microbes are living organisms that multiply and reproduce their own kind but never spontaneously generate; and that a specific kind of microbe causes a specific disease.

The basic points of germ theory may seem obvious today, but they were far from self-evident for most of human history. Until a microscope capable of revealing microorganisms was developed and used during the late seventeenth century, no one knew that microbes existed. Even then, no one suspected that such bizarre, tiny creatures could possibly affect human beings. The discovery that germs could cause disease was a painful process that was met at each stage with doubt, derision, amazement, and controversy. Early germ theorists had to demonstrate that a person did not show the symptoms of typhoid fever, for instance, unless infected with the typhoid germ. They had to prove that microbes did not suddenly appear in a formerly healthy person but came from an infecting source. They needed to determine that microbes multiplied by dividing and reproducing more of themselves in an orderly and predictable process. Furthermore, the theorists had to prove that different kinds of microbes could be identified and that, for example, a microbe that caused smallpox did not suddenly also cause cholera. All these components of germ theory had to be established before the truth of the theory could be accepted.

Once established, however, the germ theory of disease completely transformed the practice of medicine. It paved the way for new scientific disciplines such as microbiology (the study of microorganisms) and immunology (the study of the immune system and how it fights and protects against disease). It led to the prevention and treatment of diseases, epidemics, and plagues. It ultimately saved countless millions of lives and literally altered the course of history and civilization.

> **WORDS IN CONTEXT**
>
> *microorganism*
>
> An organism that can be seen only under a microscope, such as a bacterium, a protozoan, or a fungus.

Who Killed the President?

Medical knowledge of germ theory and the understanding that germs could infect people has even impacted American presidents. On July 2, 1881, for example, a mentally deranged man who thought God had told him to kill the president entered a Washington, DC, train station and shot President James A. Garfield. Garfield received two bullet wounds—one in the back and one in the arm. Neither hit any vital organs and neither was life-threatening. As a horrified and worried nation waited, a team of doctors, led by Garfield's friend, physician Willard Bliss, carried the wounded president back to the White House and attempted to treat him.

Germ theory was just beginning to be accepted during the 1880s, and many doctors in America were not believers that germs caused infection and disease. Bliss and his colleagues arrogantly and ignorantly dismissed the new theory. They poked into Garfield's wounds with dirty, unwashed hands and instruments. As the days passed they repeatedly probed the wound on his back, enlarging it and introducing

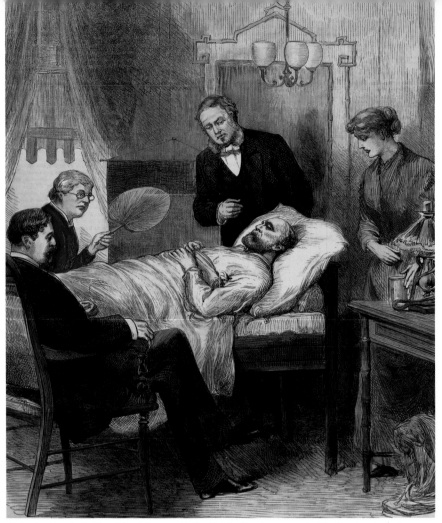

A doctor tends to President James A. Garfield after he was shot in the back and the arm in 1881. The wounds were not life-threatening, but infection resulting from unwashed hands and dirty medical instruments led to illness and death.

infection. The president developed pus in the wounds, and eventually abscesses appeared across his back. Following common treatment methods of the time, the doctors opened and drained the abscesses. Because they performed these procedures with unclean instruments, the infection spread throughout Garfield's body and bloodstream as sepsis set in. He suffered constant pain, developed high fevers, and was unable to eat or keep down any food.

Garfield's symptoms worsened over the next eighty days. By this point the small bullet hole in his back had grown into a twenty-inch-long open, oozing wound. His weight dropped from 210 pounds (95.3 kg) to 130 pounds (58.97 kg). Finally, on September 19, 1881,

Garfield grabbed his chest, cried "This pain, this pain,"[1] and died. It was not the assassin's bullets that had killed him; it was his doctors and the germs that they had unwittingly introduced into his body.

Another President Survives

One hundred years later, when the germ theory of disease had long been accepted as medical fact, another attempt on a US president's life took place. An assassin tried to kill President Ronald Reagan on March 30, 1981, but with a much different outcome. Reagan was hit by a bullet that entered under his left arm and traveled to and punctured his lung. The wound was potentially more life-threatening than Garfield's wounds had been, but Reagan survived. The surgery he required was performed under sterile, germ-free conditions, with doctors using clean instruments, washed hands covered in surgical gloves, and masks covering their mouths and noses. No infecting microbes complicated his post-surgical hospital stay. Reagan recovered fully and went on to serve two full terms as president.

> **WORDS IN CONTEXT**
>
> *sepsis*
>
> Sometimes called blood poisoning; severe inflammation that spreads throughout the body because of an infection.

Life-Saving Knowledge

In 1994 two of the medical doctors who treated Reagan, Benjamin L. Aaron and S. David Rockoff, wrote, "In 1981, President Ronald Reagan became the first incumbent president of the United States to survive being struck by a would-be assassin's bullet. Had President Reagan not survived, the history of this country and the world most certainly would have been changed."[2] No one knows in what way history might have been affected if Garfield had lived or Reagan had died, but the germ theory of disease truly changed the world for all time.

Before germ theory, untold millions died because of infections and diseases. After the advent of germ theory, millions lived because of the knowledge and treatment that germ theory made possible. At the very least, grief, fear, and suffering were dramatically diminished for people everywhere with the emergence of germ theory.

CHAPTER ONE

Before Germ Theory

The miracle windows in Trinity Chapel in Canterbury Cathedral in England were designed and erected in the early thirteenth century. These beautiful stained-glass windows depict the stories of healing miracles attributed to Thomas Beckett, the archbishop of Canterbury who was murdered there in 1170 CE. Within days after the holy man's murder, according to the records of the time, miracles of healing occurred in the cathedral. Soon after his death the archbishop was declared a saint by the Catholic Church. Throughout Europe's Middle Ages people suffering with diseases and injuries made religious journeys, or pilgrimages, to St. Thomas's shrine to pray for the saint's help and a miracle cure of their own. The miracle windows portray forty-two of their stories, including, for instance, the healing of Ethelreda of Canterbury. She was stricken with the fever and debilitation of malaria. At St. Thomas's tomb within the shrine, she prays to the saint and drinks a bowl of water tinged with a drop of the martyred man's blood and is cured of her disease. Other panels in the windows show Godwin of Boxgrove cured of his leprosy (now known as Hansen's disease) and a woman healed of dropsy (an old term for edema or the buildup of fluid in the body). In one panel a bedridden monk is shown surrounded by physicians and surgeons who can do nothing for him until the monk drinks holy water from St. Thomas's shrine and is cured. An early chant written at Canterbury goes:

> Thomas shines with new miracles,
> endows with male parts those who are castrated,
> provides vision to those deprived of eyes.
> Cleans those spattered with the spots of leprosy,
> loosens those bound with the chains of death.[3]

God's Will

The Catholic Church and almost all people during the Middle Ages believed that disease and disability were punishments from God and that the best hope for a cure lay in repenting one's sins and begging a saint for help. No one had any idea of what caused disease, or how to prevent it, or how to heal it. Prayer and offerings to God were often the best hope that sick people had. In the Christian world, in the Muslim world, in Asia, and in Africa, priests and physicians regularly blamed diseases that seemed to strike for no reason on God, evil or angry spirits, or the devil and witchcraft. Potions, prayers, chants, and spells were the treatments of choice. An ancient Egyptian cure, for example, combines a potion of herbs with the spell, "Come! You who drives out evil things from my stomach and my limbs. He who drinks this shall be cured just as the gods above were cured."[4]

In Western Europe—where the germ theory of disease would eventually arise—the supernatural explanation of disease did not

A close-up view from Trinity Chapel's stained-glass miracle windows depicts a priest's attempt to revive a victim of the plague with holy water. According to the tale, the victim was miraculously cured.

preclude the emergence of medicine and physicians. These educated people turned to ancient Greek and Roman writings to understand the practical, natural reasons for disease. The physical explanation of disease that was accepted from ancient times until the nineteenth century is known as humoral theory. It was originally described by Hippocrates in about the fourth century BCE and elaborated in the second century CE by the Greek physician Galen. Humoral theory states that the body is made up of four humors, or fluids, that must be in balance to maintain health. These humors are black bile, yellow bile, phlegm, and blood. An imbalance in these fluids leads to disease,

Seedlets of Disease

In the sixteenth century the Italian philosopher, mathematician, and physician Girolamo Fracastoro wrote a long poem titled *De Contagione et Contagiosis Morbis et Eorum Curatione* (On Contagion and Contagious Diseases and Their Cure). In his book Fracastoro describes several contagious diseases and his theories about how the diseases are passed from person to person through "seeds of contagion." He proposes that tiny, unseen particles—or seedlets—of disease could be infectious in three different ways: The seedlets could sicken someone in direct contact with a disease victim. Or they could be lying in the clothing, bed linen, or wooden belongings of the disease victim and then passed to another person who touched these objects. Or they could infect someone at a distance, perhaps through the air. Fracastoro's ideas were in direct contradiction to miasma theory and to Galen, and critics attacked him for such a ridiculous fantasy. One physician called Fracastoro "our foolish and stupid friend from Verona."

Fracastoro's theories of contagion remained unappreciated and fell into oblivion until the nineteenth century when germ theorists rediscovered his writings and praised him for his forward thinking. He came closer than anyone before him to the truth about infection and microbes—and long before any evidence of the existence of germs was even possible.

Quoted in Robert P. Gaynes, *Germ Theory: Medical Pioneers in Infectious Diseases*. Kindle edition. Washington, DC: ASM, 2011.

so treatment consists of bleeding the patient or purging him or her with enemas or emetics to cause vomiting in order to bring the humors back into balance.

The humoral theory meant that sickness came from inside the body, not an outside agent or outside events, unless these events were God's decisions. Since medical treatments of sick people by cutting and bleeding them or forcing them to vomit did no good and often made people worse, praying for a miracle or God's forgiveness was frequently a better option for fighting disease than the medical cures of the time. Throughout Europe and the Arab world Galen's humoral theory was accepted along with theories that plagues and epidemics came from God. Nevertheless, some understanding that at least a few diseases were contagious and could spread from person to person did exist during the Middle Ages.

Thinking About Contagion

During the medieval era Arab civilization and learning far surpassed Europe's. In the eleventh century a scholarly Persian physician named Abu Ali al-Husayn Ibn Sina (known in Europe as Avicenna) became one of the first people in the world to try to describe contagion as a cause of disease. Ibn Sina is considered the father of modern medicine, and his text *Canon of Medicine* was used in medical schools in Europe and around the world for six hundred years. Ibn Sina believed in the humoral theory of Hippocrates and Galen, but he also recorded his own observations, experiences, and conclusions about disease and medicine in general. He was the first person in the world to suggest that *phthisis* (the ancient word for tuberculosis) might be contagious. In one section of Ibn Sina's large medical book, he writes, "Very often, too, the air itself is the seat of the beginning of the decomposition changes [the wasting away of the body from tuberculosis]—either because it is contaminated by adjoining impure air, or by some 'celestial' agent of a quality at present unknown to man."[5]

Hundreds of years before the invention of the microscope, Ibn Sina could have had no idea of what might be in the air that could infect a body, but he was proposing a cause of the disease that was external to the body rather than an internal imbalance. Ibn Sina also suggested that sexual diseases were contagious and wrote that some worms and parasites could cause disease. He thought that some parasitical diseases could arise from drinking or bathing in dirty water or from the soil. He was the first person to recommend quarantine (isolating a person to restrict contact with others) as a way to prevent the spread of tuberculosis in the population.

Plague: Contagion or God's Plan?

In Europe, despite the widespread use of Ibn Sina's book in medical schools, the idea of the contagiousness of disease was not accepted. Physicians continued to rely on the humoral theory of disease and on their belief that epidemics came from God. When bubonic plague struck Eurasia in the middle of the fourteenth century, however, people did recognize that it was contagious but did not understand how or why. Although originally carried by fleas on infected rats, one form of the plague was easily spread by people, and few survived once infected. The symptoms of plague were gruesome. People developed high fevers, vomiting, and bloody coughs. Black tumors called buboes spread over the victim's body and oozed pus and blood. Doctors could neither explain the cause nor treat the symptoms. People who were able escaped areas where the plague struck, and others avoided and abandoned neighbors and family members who were stricken.

Physicians attempted to treat the victims with bloodletting and draining the buboes. Some medical experts of the time offered astrological explanations for the plague, such as the alignment of planets in the sky creating evil vapors on Earth that were breathed in by the victims. One doctor in Europe explained that "instantaneous death occurs when the aerial spirit escaping from the eyes of the sick man strikes the healthy person standing near and looking at the sick."[6]

WORDS IN CONTEXT

vapors

Gaseous substances suspended in the air that may be foul-smelling or poisonous.

In Christian Europe most people saw the plague as divine punishment for humanity's sins; therefore, people were helpless against it. In the Islamic world, plague was also viewed as coming from God,

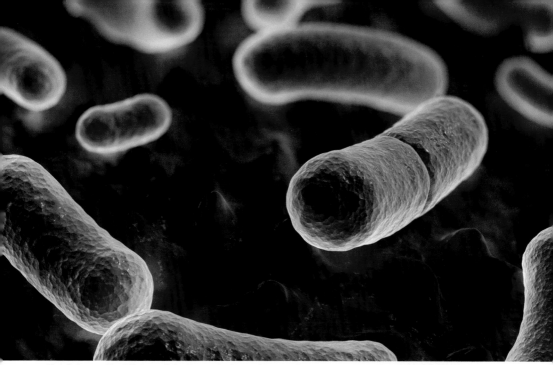

Yersinia pestis *(pictured)* is the rod-shaped bacterium responsible for the plague that killed millions during the Middle Ages. Knowing nothing of bacteria or other germs, doctors of this era resorted to bloodletting and other measures that had no effect on the course of the disease.

but Islamic scholars and doctors did not believe that God punished good Muslims with disease. Instead, they saw the plague as a mercy from God that allowed people to go to heaven. The Prophet Muhammad had once said, "Disease is not the wrath of Allah, because Prophets also suffered great pains, much greater than ordinary people."[7] So victims of epidemics and plagues were not sinners but martyrs to their faith. In both worlds, however, contagion and plague were simply viewed as part of God's plan.

Miasma Theory

As the Islamic world declined through outside invasions during the thirteenth century and ongoing internal dissensions, medical progress stalled. Then, as Europe entered the Renaissance era of the fifteenth to seventeenth centuries, respect for Arab medicine diminished. Reaching back to the classical Greek and Roman civilizations for inspiration, educated people during the Renaissance rejected Arab learning and adhered even more strongly to ancient Greek theories of disease. They ignored Ibn Sina's discussions of contagion and clung to Galen's humoral theory, but they did expand on the idea that bad air was the cause of many diseases. This tainted air affected individuals differently, depending on the balance of their humors, and that was why some people got sick during epidemics and others did not. While they searched for explanations other than God, Renaissance physicians blamed evil air and winds as the cause of epidemics.

By the seventeenth or eighteenth century this approach became known and accepted as the miasma theory of disease. According to the Science Museum of London, "In miasma theory, diseases were caused by the presence in the air of a miasma, a poisonous vapour in which were suspended particles of decaying matter that was characterised by its foul smell."[8] Miasmas could come from decaying animal or plant materials, swamps and marshes, stagnant water, stinking garbage dumps, cesspools and human waste sites, or even from earthquakes that released poisoned gases into the air. The miasma theory of disease led to an effort to clean up the commonly filthy cities in Europe. For example, one Renaissance architect in 1450 wrote of the importance of constructing sewer systems for "preserving the wholesomeness and purity of the air."[9] The miasmic theory did help European peoples to avoid some germs, such as those that spread from exposed human feces. It partially protected people from some contagious diseases. Medical understanding of disease causation, however, did not advance, and many diseases remained rampant.

WORDS IN CONTEXT

miasma

An oppressive, unhealthy atmosphere, dangerous vapor, or poisonous, polluted air.

Diseases Everywhere

In Europe in the eighteenth century, for example, smallpox was an endemic disease, meaning it occurred regularly and frequently. It caused high fevers, vomiting and diarrhea, and an eruption of pustules (pox) on the skin. Up to 30 percent of people who developed smallpox died, and those who survived were often left with pitted, disfiguring scars where the pustules had healed. In children younger than five years old the disease was especially devastating: At least 80 percent of those who contracted smallpox died. The English historian Thomas Macauley writes, "Smallpox was always present, filling the churchyard with corpses, tormenting with constant fear all of whom it had not yet stricken, leaving on those whose lives it spared the hideous traces of its power, turning the babe into a changeling at which the mother shuddered, and making the eyes and cheeks of the betrothed maiden objects of horror to the lover."[10]

Smallpox, however, was far from the only disease threat faced by eighteenth-century people. Tuberculosis, a disease of the lungs called the White Plague because of its victims' pale, wasted appearance, was a leading cause of death. Epidemics of dysentery and cholera (both diarrheal diseases), typhoid (spread by contaminated feces), and typhus (spread by lice and fleas and causing high fever with severe muscle pain) regularly devastated communities. Infectious diseases of all kinds were the leading cause of death in people of all ages and were mainly responsible for limiting life expectancies in Europe between 1500 and 1800 to somewhere between thirty and forty years old. Medicine offered little hope against disease, and people lived in fear and helplessness, never knowing when disease would strike.

The Discovery of the Microscopic World

No one suspected that germs might be the cause of disease. Not until the invention of the first microscope powerful enough to see microorganisms was germ theory even possible. The person who invented that microscope was Antonie van Leeuwenhoek of the Netherlands. He was not an educated scientist but a shopkeeper and janitor in city hall.

He was fascinated, however, when he saw one of the primitive, handheld microscopes that had already been developed. It had no more power than a modern magnifying glass, but Van Leeuwenhoek was inspired to make a better one. He learned the process of grinding lenses and eventually developed a process that let him magnify two hundred times and, with patience and carefulness, still see clearly. He became the first person in the world to see bacteria and other single-celled organisms. It was an astounding discovery. In 1674 Van Leeuwenhoek looked at a drop of pond water through his microscope and saw the single-celled animals known as protozoa. He wrote about the tiny living creatures to the scientists and philosophers who formed the Royal Society of London saying, "Their belly was flat provided with divers [several] incredibly thin little feet or little legs, which ever moved very nimbly, and which I was able to discover only after sundry great efforts, and wherein they brought off incredibly quick motions."[11]

In 1683 Van Leeuwenhoek discovered bacteria by examining his saliva and scrapings from his teeth. In another letter to the Royal Society, he wrote the world's first description of bacteria, which he named "animalcules," or tiny animals. He said of the material from his mouth, "I then most always saw, with great wonder, that in the said matter there were many very little living animalcules, very prettily a-moving. The biggest sort . . . had a very strong and swift motion, and shot through the water (or spittle) like a pike does through the water. The second sort . . . oft-times spun round like a top . . . and these were far more in number."[12]

The incredible discovery of a microscopic world stunned and amazed the learned scientists of the Royal Society. Many of them

Van Leeuwenhoek's Microscopes

No matter how often he was asked, Van Leeuwenhoek never gave away even one of his microscopes nor explained to anyone how he made them. One member of the Royal Society of London, the philosopher Gottfried Wilhelm Leibniz, was so impressed by what he saw through the microscopes that he begged Van Leeuwenhoek to teach students the skill of lens making. Otherwise, said Leibniz, the ability would be lost, and research into the microscopic world would cease. Van Leeuwenhoek refused, saying that he could not be a slave to students. Royal Society member William Molyneux begged to be allowed to buy just one of hundreds of microscopes so that scientists might make use of it. His plea was rejected.

During his lifetime Van Leeuwenhoek wrote hundreds of letters to the Royal Society, describing everything he discovered of the microscopic world. The members were so impressed that they elected him to membership in 1680. Nevertheless, he maintained his secrecy about his microscopes until his death in 1723 at the age of ninety-one. In his will, however, he bequeathed twenty-six of his microscopes to the Royal Society of London.

Antonie van Leeuwenhoek peers through the microscope that allowed him to see bacteria and other single-celled organisms. The improvements he made to the microscope's lenses magnified images well beyond what other instruments of the period could do.

visited the Netherlands to see the marvels for themselves, but Van Leeuwenhoek was a secretive and suspicious man who allowed visitors to look through but never touch his microscopes. He refused to explain how he made his microscopes and would not give away even one of his own. He became famous for his discovery of the strange, microscopic world that shared Earth with humanity, but it was a curiosity only. No one suspected that such insignificant, tiny creatures could affect people in any way. Almost no one studied them because no one had a quality microscope that could see microorganisms. Medical professionals certainly had no interest in microscopes or animalcules. Even when powerful microscopes finally came into general use in the nineteenth century, no one put microorganisms together with the onset of sickness and disease. For more than 150 years no one recognized the importance of what Van Leeuwenhoek called his "wretched beasties,"[13] but the door had been opened, and during the nineteenth century other scientists finally walked through it.

CHAPTER TWO

The Celebrated Founders of Germ Theory

Even the greatest and most creative of innovators builds on the work of others. The atmosphere of science and reason fostered during the eighteenth and nineteenth centuries encouraged medical investigation. As physicians learned about human anatomy and physiology, the humoral theory was finally discredited. In the eighteenth century Giovanni Battista Morgagni, for example, used his observations from more than seven hundred autopsies to proclaim to the medical world, "Signs and symptoms are the cry of the suffering organs within!"[14] In other words, symptoms of illness—for example chest pains and heart attacks—were correlated with damage to a specific organ— in this example, the heart. Balance of humors had nothing to do with disease symptoms. Neither was balancing humors necessary to protect people from disease. In 1796 Edward Jenner proved that cowpox, a mild disease, protected against smallpox, a devastating disease. He used the fluid from cowpox pustules on infected people to develop the world's first vaccine—a vaccine against smallpox.

The enthusiasm for scientific investigation also led to the development of quality microscopes in the nineteenth century, which allowed scientists to view and study microbes. In 1837 Theodor Schwann discovered that microbes were the cause of meat spoiling and becoming rotten. Schwann's microscopic studies revealed "wriggling, cavorting creatures a thousand times smaller than a pinhead—it is these beasts that make meat go bad."[15] At the same time, researcher Charles Cagniard de la Tour discovered that yeasts are alive and responsible for the fermentation of alcohol.

The scientific world was close to understanding that microbes play an important role in human life, but it took French chemist Louis Pasteur to put all the clues together and develop the germ theory of disease. Pasteur was the originator of germ theory, but ultimately its proof fell to German physician Robert Koch. The application of germ theory to medical practice was accomplished by another man, English surgeon Joseph Lister. These three men were the founders of modern medicine.

Edward Jenner inoculates a child against smallpox. He used the fluid from cowpox pustules to develop the world's first vaccine.

Spontaneous Generation

In the mid-nineteenth century scientists argued intensely about spontaneous generation. Everyone knew that boiling milk or beef broth killed all microbial life. Let that same milk or broth sit for a day or two, and it was teeming with microorganisms. Many researchers held to the theory that microbes simply appeared in the fluid, created from nothing but the nonliving material itself and perhaps exposure to the air. Living microbes arose, or were spontaneously generated, from inanimate material.

If this theory were true, the idea of contagious diseases caused by microbes was meaningless. Microbes could just appear anywhere and in any person for no reason. Pasteur had to prove those theorists wrong. He devised an experiment in which he placed a rich broth in a swan-neck flask. The thin neck of the flask was shaped like an S. First Pasteur boiled the broth until it was completely free of microorganisms. Then he allowed the flask to sit in the open air in his laboratory and waited to see if microbes would appear. Air could get into the flask, but the shape of the flask's neck prevented the entrance of any dust motes or microscopic particles suspended in the air. They were trapped in the curve of the swan-neck. The broth remained pure, with no sign of microbes. Pasteur had conclusively refuted the theory of spontaneous generation, and he was able to assert that microbes never "came into the world without germs, without parents similar to themselves."

Quoted in Robert P. Gaynes, *Germ Theory: Medical Pioneers in Infectious Diseases.* Kindle edition. Washington, DC: ASM, 2011.

Louis Pasteur

Born in Dole, France, in 1822, Louis Pasteur became a professor of chemistry at the University of Lille in 1854. In business-oriented Lille were many distilleries that produced alcohol from beet sugar. When the father of one of Pasteur's students asked for help in figuring out why so many of his vats failed to make alcohol, Pasteur eagerly accepted the challenge. He knew nothing about fermentation or alcohol production, but he was skilled at using a microscope because of his chemistry background. Pasteur discovered that millions of rod-shaped, wriggling microbes had infected the failed brewery vats, so that no fermentation could take place. Instead, the brew in these vats turned sour with the same acid that was in sour milk. At the same time, rapidly multiplying living yeasts were turning sugar into alcohol in the healthy vats. With a great leap of logic, Pasteur conceptualized his germ theory: if alcohol could suffer from a disease caused by microbes, he speculated, perhaps animals and people, too, could become diseased from invading germs. Historian and microbiologist Paul de Kruif says, "His experiment with the little rods that made the acid of sour milk convinced him—why, no one can tell—that other kinds of small beings did a thousand other gigantic and useful and perhaps dangerous things in the world."[16]

In 1857 Pasteur moved to Paris and continued his research into fermentation. He developed pasteurization—the process of slow heating to kill unwanted microbes that caused the diseases of wine, beer, cider, vinegar, and eventually milk. During the 1860s he single-handedly saved France's silkworm industry, which was close to ruin because of a disease that was killing the silkworms. He discovered two microbes that were sickening the silkworms and showed the plantation owners how to identify and separate the sick worms from the healthy ones.

Pasteur became absolutely convinced that microbes cause disease in animals and in humans. During the 1870s he wrote scientific papers, gave speeches, and offered public presentations about his germ theory. He was a charismatic and compelling man. Once, he gave a speech during which he shined a bright light in the dark theater and warned, "Observe the thousands of dancing specks of dust in the path of this ray. The air of this hall is filled with these specks of dust, these thousands of little nothings that you should not despise always [belittle], for sometimes they carry disease and death; the typhus, the cholera, the yellow fever and many other pestilences!"[17] He thrilled the public with his persuasiveness and convinced not only much of the public but also many scientists of the correctness of his germ theory.

Germ Theory and the Development of Vaccines

Always believing that science should benefit society, Pasteur researched farm animal diseases and grew microbes in nutrient-rich broths that he could inject into lab animals to see if they became sick. While experimenting with these broths, he had the fortunate accident of forgetting one for several days and letting it dry out. The microbes in this old broth were weakened, or attenuated. They did not make his lab animals sick. Pasteur always said, "In the fields of observation chance favors the prepared mind."[18] Realizing that microbes could be weakened led Pasteur to the theory that attenuated microbes might be used as vaccines that would make an animal immune to the actual disease. He developed a vaccine for chicken cholera for chickens and then a vaccine for the deadly anthrax microbe that often decimated cattle, goat, and sheep herds.

WORDS IN CONTEXT

attenuated

Altered and weakened so that the infectious agent is alive but harmless.

Pasteur next turned his attention to developing a vaccine for humans. He chose rabies, then a horrifyingly common disease that killed anyone bitten by an infected animal and caused much suffering, fear, and torment. Pasteur could not find the germ that causes rabies because it is much smaller than the germs that cause anthrax or chicken cholera. The anthrax and chicken cholera germs are bacteria. The rabies germ is a virus, and it is too small to be seen with the strongest light microscope. Nevertheless, Pasteur was sure that a germ was responsible. He developed an attenuated vaccine from the crushed-up spinal cords of infected dogs. Since it takes about a month for the rabies virus to work its way to the victim's brain and spinal cord, the vaccine—given in gradually increasing dosage strengths—could protect a patient even after he or she was bitten by a rabid animal. Immunity was established before the virus infected the victim.

On July 6, 1885, nine-year-old Joseph Meister was bitten by a rabid dog and received the first treatment with Pasteur's rabies vaccine. Fourteen days later, the boy became the first person ever known to survive a rabies attack and went home completely healthy. Around the world, Pasteur was hailed as a hero. Within fifteen months he had treated 2,490 people, including nineteen Russian peasants attacked by rabid wolves and a fifteen-year-old French boy. In his honor, grateful heads of state and ordinary citizens donated money to build the Pasteur Institute in Paris where he would work for the rest of his life.

Robert Koch

Despite the success of his vaccines, Pasteur was unable to prove conclusively that germ theory was true. That task was accomplished by a younger contemporary—Robert Koch of Germany. Born in 1843, Koch was a country doctor who became fascinated with microorganisms when his wife gave him a microscope as a birthday present. Koch served in Germany's army as a physician during the Franco-German War and became increasingly disturbed by his inability to help soldiers suffering with infections and diseases. After the war, during the 1870s, Koch devoted himself to microscopic studies in a makeshift laboratory where he used mice and bacterial cultures in an effort to determine with certainty that germs cause disease. Pasteur insisted that different bacteria caused specific disease symptoms, but Koch wanted scientific proof.

One of the major problems at the time was that bacteria did not show up clearly enough under the microscope for researchers to distinguish among different kinds. Koch discovered that aniline dyes (made from coal tar) could stain bacteria. The bacteria absorbed the dye while any surrounding tissue did not. The shape and form of dyed bacteria were clear. Koch could easily identify different bacterial species and even photograph them. Then he developed a method of isolating pure cultures of just one kind of bacteria, using relatively large anthrax bacteria. Now he could inject pure cultures of anthrax bacteria into his laboratory mice and demonstrate that anthrax bacteria and anthrax bacteria alone caused the disease to develop.

Koch's rigorous work earned him recognition from the scientific community, and in 1880 he received an appointment as director of Berlin's Imperial Health Office, with a staff and laboratory. There he learned to use a gelatin beef mixture to grow pure bacterial cultures. One of his assistants, Julius Richard Petri, developed a small, shallow dish for the purpose, which was forever after called the petri dish. In 1881, when Koch traveled to London to demonstrate his staining and growth

Koch's Postulates

In 1877 Robert Koch published his scientific criteria for demonstrating that specific germs cause specific diseases that can reproduce and spread from one animal to another. The criteria introduced by Koch are known as Koch's postulates. According to the postulates: **(1)** The suspected germ, or pathogen, must be present in all cases of the illness. **(2)** The pathogen can be obtained from the diseased host and cultured in a lab. **(3)** The culture must cause the disease when injected into a healthy laboratory animal. **(4)** Once isolated from that animal, the pathogen proves to be the same as the original one.

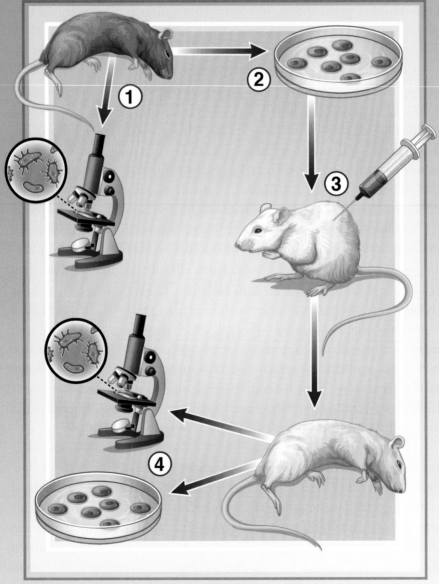

Source: Michigan State University, "Koch's Postulates." www.msu.edu.

techniques, he met Pasteur and Lister. Both men were impressed, but it was the last time that Pasteur and Koch had a cordial conversation. As Koch's scientific investigations progressed, he criticized Pasteur for lack of rigor in experimentation, and the two men became enemies. The hostility was perhaps exaggerated by the patriotism of both men and their conflicting loyalties during the Franco-German War.

Koch's proofs that specific microbes caused specific diseases were based on a set of principles that any scientist could follow. Known as Koch's postulates, the principles are:

1. The microbe is present in each case of the disease.
2. The microbe can be taken from the infected host and grown independently.
3. The disease can be produced by introducing a pure culture of the microbe into a healthy host.
4. The microbe can be isolated and identified from the host infected in Step 3.[19]

Discovering the Cause of Tuberculosis

In 1881 Koch followed his postulates to identify the microbe that causes tuberculosis (TB). At that time one out of every seven deaths of every man, woman, and child in Europe and America was due to TB, which many doctors believed to be inherited. Koch experimented with different dyes until he found one called methylene blue that stained the tiny curved rods that are TB bacteria. He collected his first sample from a laborer who had died from the disease. He grew pure cultures of the microbes in the lab, injected them into guinea pigs, took samples from their dead bodies, grew those samples again in his dishes, and finally determined that those microbes, too, could kill other guinea pigs. Ultimately, he discovered that the germs could be sprayed into the air of a box of guinea pigs and infect them with TB. Now he knew not only that TB was caused by a specific microbe but also how the infection spread through the air.

On March 24, 1882, Koch presented his findings to the scientists at the Berlin Physiological Society and was immediately acclaimed as a hero by medical professionals and the public at large. The *New York Times* announced Koch's presentation to be "one of the great scientific discoveries of the age."[20] Scientists from around the world flocked to

Koch's laboratory to learn microbe hunting from him. His stature increased in 1883, when he discovered the bacterium that causes cholera.

Joseph Lister

Koch dedicated himself to proving that specific microbes cause specific diseases. Pasteur had concentrated on attenuating microbes in order to develop vaccines. Lister, the third founder of germ theory, used germ theory to prove that killing microbes saves lives.

Lister, a Quaker surgeon, was born in England in 1827. His father, Joseph Jackson Lister, invented the modern light microscope, so Lister was familiar with microscopy from childhood. In Lister's time more than 50 percent of surgeries ended in the death of the patient, and infections were generally expected after any surgical procedure. Physicians did not know what caused infections, but they described different "putrefaction" syndromes. Patients might develop septicemia (infection in the bloodstream), pyemia (fever accompanied by a wound oozing pus), erysipelas (blisters, fever, and red skin and rash), gangrene (death of body tissue and flesh), and tetanus (infection of the nervous system). The generally accepted explanation for all these syndromes was that oxygen in the air attacked open wounds and caused these unpreventable complications.

In 1860 Lister was working in Glasgow, Scotland, and happened to read Pasteur's papers about the diseases of fermentation caused by microbes. Fascinated, Lister read the articles over and over and speculated that germs could be causing putrefaction in surgical patients just as they caused diseases in wine and beer. He used his microscope to determine that microbes were indeed present in his patients' wounds, and that realization marked his conversion to germ theory. He later explained, "All efforts to combat decomposition of the blood in open wounds were in vain until Pasteur's researches opened a new way, by combating the microbes."[21]

Lister could not fight the microbes by killing them with heat as Pasteur had done with pasteurization, so he looked for a chemical means to kill germs. He chose carbolic acid, a derivative of coal tar then used to reduce smells in open sewers. It was strong and irritated the skin; it also killed microbes. He tried it first on an eleven-year-old boy with a compound fracture of his leg, in which the bone had

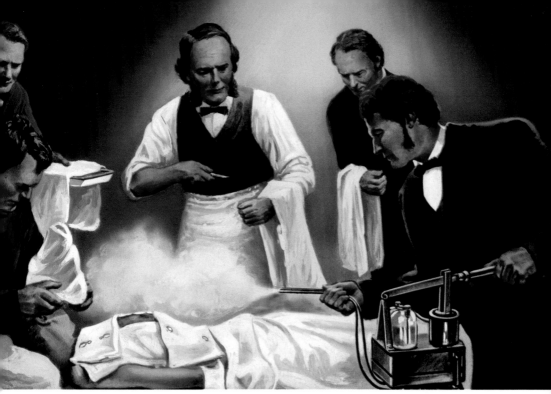

Joseph Lister uses a carbolic acid sprayer to disinfect the air inside an operating room before doctors begin surgery. Lister found that this and other germ-killing methods dramatically reduced patient mortality in hospitals.

pierced the skin and created an open wound. Lister first set the bone, then poured carbolic acid over the wound, and finally pressed a bandage soaked in carbolic acid over the wound and wrapped the whole thing in foil. The boy's leg healed beautifully, with no sign of infection. Several more treatments of compound fractures thereafter proved to Lister that killing microbes saved lives and limbs. It was not oxygen but microbes that caused infections.

Listerian Surgery

When Lister applied his germ-killing methods to surgical procedures and wounds, he achieved the same remarkable success. He became zealous about antisepsis—killing any germs present before, during, and after surgery. He washed his hands in carbolic acid, cleaned instruments with it, developed a carbolic acid sprayer to kill any germs in the operating room air, and dressed post-surgical wounds in soaked bandages. By 1870 he was able to report in a medical article that his antiseptic surgical methods had dramatically reduced mortality at his hospital. Before antisepsis, the death rate after surgery was one death in every 2.5 cases. After he instituted antiseptic surgery, mortality dropped to one death in every 6.5 cases. Lister set out his essential conditions for successful surgery as follows:

1. The first thing that has to be done is to destroy the germs on the patient's skin, on the surgeon's hands, on the instruments which are to be used and on everything surrounding the area of operation.
2. The second is to prevent living germs from entering the wound from the air or the surrounding objects during the performance of the operation.
3. And the third is to prevent germs from spreading into the wound after the operation.[22]

Lister was an ardent believer in germ theory, and he set out to convince the medical world of the importance of Listerian surgery. Because of the thousands of wounded soldiers during the Franco-German War doctors in Germany and France were desperate to try anything to save lives, and they quickly became converts. Doctors in England and the United States, however, were slow to believe. Listerian surgery was tedious and complicated, and doctors sneered at microbes and were offended by the idea that physicians carried infectious germs. Lister toured the United States to promote his methods and then accepted a surgical post in England, where he treated Queen Victoria of England for an abscess in her armpit while her personal physician worked the carbolic acid sprayer. By 1880 many doctors accepted germ theory, but it was not accepted in America until after President James A. Garfield died of infection carried on the hands of his physicians. In England, only the continued success of Listerian surgery in London gradually persuaded doctors that germ theory was correct.

Germ Theory Has Triumphed

Throughout his later years Lister was honored for his accomplishments, but he credited Pasteur, explaining that the previous horrors

Fighting for Science

Louis Pasteur was passionate about germ theory and did not handle op-position well. In 1881, when he was sixty years old and had success-fully developed his chicken cholera vaccine, he attended a meeting of the Academy of Medicine and not only described the vaccine and its effects but also boasted that his discovery was more important than Edward Jen-ner's development of the smallpox vaccine. He had shown what Jenner did not—that microbes both cause disease and at the same time can be weakened and used to prevent the same disease.

The traditional doctors of the Academy of Medicine were offended. Jenner was a medical hero and Pasteur a mere chemist. The eighty-year-old physician Jules Guerin sneered at Pasteur for making such a big deal about silly chickens. Enraged, Pasteur yelled that Guerin's treatment methods and medical approaches were stupid nonsense. Guerin tottered toward Pasteur and tried to attack him. A fist fight was averted only be-cause other academy members rushed to pull the two men apart. The next day, Guerin challenged Pasteur to a duel for the slurs on his honor and ability. Pasteur backed down and sent a message to the Academy retracting his criticisms of Guerin. He wrote, "I am ready . . . to modify whatever the editors may consider as going beyond the rights of criticism and legitimate defense." It was an apology of sorts, but the incident dem-onstrates the emotional furor that was caused by Pasteur's insistence that medicine accept the germ theory of disease.

Quoted in Paul de Kruif, *Microbe Hunters*. New York: Houghton Mifflin Harcourt, 1926, p. 148.

of surgery had disappeared only because of Pasteur's germ theory. In his speech at Pasteur's retirement ceremony, Lister said, "M. Pasteur, infectious diseases constitute, as you know, the greater number of the maladies to which the human race is subject. You can therefore well understand why it is that on this impressive occasion medicine and surgery hasten to bring to you the profound homage of their admira-tion and gratitude."[23] Koch was not present at the celebration; the old hostility held. Nevertheless, history remembers all three men as the germ theorists who changed medicine and human health forever.

CHAPTER THREE

The Revolution in Medicine

The impact of germ theory on medical science and practice was profound. Scientists and medical researchers embraced germ theory, immersed themselves in the new discipline of microbiology, and leaped forward in their understanding of germs and disease. By the 1890s excited, optimistic researchers searched for disease-causing microbes, and the prestige of the medical profession rose dramatically as doctors used discoveries to employ diagnostic, treatment, and prevention methods that actually worked. The period from 1857 (when Louis Pasteur formulated germ theory) to 1914 is sometimes called the Golden Age of Microbiology. With germ theory established, eager scientists flocked to the Pasteur Institute and Robert Koch's laboratories for training. Germ theory made it possible for them and other researchers to make rapid progress in identifying specific microbes, determining how diseases were transmitted, and understanding how to avoid or prevent disease.

Understanding and Preventing Infections

With the acceptance of germ theory came the great incentive to study the world of microbes in detail. Researchers sought to learn how microbes lived, what kinds there were, how they infected hosts, what properties they had that allowed them to multiply and sicken people, and what medicine could do to thwart them. During the 1890s, for example, physicians not only accepted Joseph Lister's antiseptic theories of wound treatment but gradually improved upon them. Asepsis became the surgical norm, and physicians learned to sterilize instruments, wear caps, gowns, gloves, and masks during surgery; formulate milder antiseptics than carbolic acid; and work in germ-free, easily cleaned operating rooms.

As physicians learned that thorough hand washing removed many microbes, they not only made surgery safer but also eliminated one of the greatest dangers of childbirth—puerperal fever. More commonly called childbed fever, puerperal fever was a life-threatening complication of childbirth. Caused by the bacteria carried on doctors' hands and dirty instruments as they moved from surgical patients to diseased patients to autopsies to delivering a baby, the infection killed five out of every thousand women in Europe in the first half of the nineteenth century. By 1900 germ theory and hand washing made the infection a rarity as doctors finally accepted that they were the culprits behind the mysterious fever.

The realization that germs caused surgical and childbirth infections made scientists ask what other infections were caused by which specific microbes. In 1883, for instance, Friedrich Fehleisen collected the pus from the rashes of patients with erysipelas and discovered through microscopic examination that the germs looked like little balls joined together by a string. He was the first person to identify these microbes—later named *streptococcus*, or strep, bacteria. For some reason unknown today, Fehleisen thought these strep bacteria might cure cancer and injected them into cancer patients. When each of these patients came down with erysipelas, Fehleisen had proof that strep is the specific cause of this specific infection (although this was not the outcome he was after).

WORDS IN CONTEXT

asepsis
Preventing microorganisms from contaminating the environment by maintaining sterile conditions.

In those early days of germ theory, researchers performed some shockingly unreasonable and dangerous experiments. Carl Alois Philipp Garre injected a test tube full of microbes isolated from a boil into his own arm. He wanted to know if it was true that the microbes alone were the cause of this infection. Boils are skin abscesses full of the pus-forming bacteria known as *staphylococcus* bacteria, or staph. Garre injected such an overdose into his arm that he developed a huge carbuncle (a large lump of several boils together) and twenty separate boils. He did not care about the pain and misery he caused himself.

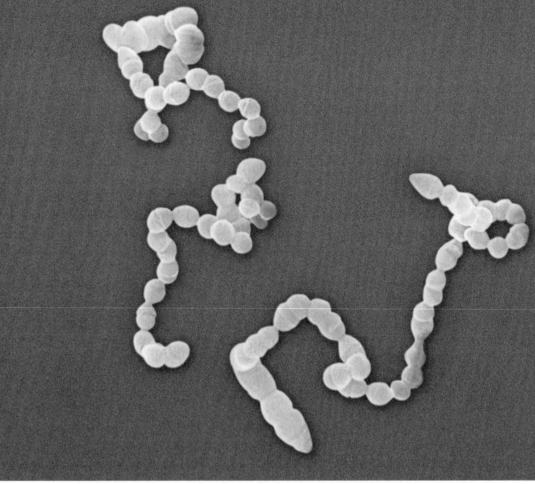

Streptococcus *bacteria (pictured) were identified in 1883 as the cause of a skin infection known as erysipelas. That connection was made by a doctor who was searching for a cure for cancer.*

Instead, he reveled, "I now know that this microbe, this staphylococcus, is the true cause of boils and carbuncles!"[24]

Identifying Disease Bacteria

Recognizing the bacteria that cause specific diseases was just as exciting to scientists as identifying staph and strep bacteria as causes of skin and wound infections. And the recognition came rapidly. By 1900, researchers from the Pasteur Institute in Paris and Koch's Institute for Infectious Diseases in Berlin had identified twenty-one different microbes that caused specific diseases. In 1890, for example, Pierre Paul Émile Roux (who taught the world's first microbiology course) and Alexandre Yersin of the Pasteur Institute proved for the first time that diphtheria—a killer respiratory disease of childhood—was caused by a bacterium. Furthermore, they discovered that the bacteria produced a toxin, or poison, that caused the disease symptoms even when the bacteria had all died. In 1894 Yersin traveled to Hong Kong to study an outbreak there of bubonic plague. Yersin isolated microbes from the buboes of infected dead patients and proved through laboratory animal experiments that the germs cause the disease. In his honor the bacterium was later named *Yersinia pestis*. In 1889 Japanese-born Shibasaburo Kitasato, who was trained by Koch at his Institute, isolated and grew a pure culture of the small, rod-shaped bacteria that cause tetanus. Kitasato then discovered that these microbes produced a toxin, or poison, that was responsible for the symptoms of tetanus. In 1898 he discovered the microbe that causes the diarrheal disease of dysentery, as well.

The Beginning of Immunology

The insight that some microbes produce toxins was groundbreaking, because it gave scientists a medical way to fight microbes based on what they were manufacturing in the body. Kitasato injected small amounts of tetanus toxins (not the bacteria themselves) into lab animals which then developed antibodies in their blood that protected them from full doses of tetanus bacteria. From this work he developed the world's first tetanus vaccine. Kitasato also helped fellow researcher Emil von Behring use the discovery of diphtheria toxins to develop an antitoxin serum therapy for children, thousands of whom died in epidemics every year from the contagious respiratory disease known as the strangling angel.

Von Behring, also at Koch's Institute, discovered that small amounts of the diphtheria toxins injected into animals did not kill them. Instead, it resulted in the formation of antibodies in the animals' blood. Antibodies are proteins formed in response to an infection by a specific microbe or any substance that the body recognizes as a foreign invader. Once manufactured, antibodies remain in the blood, ready to signal the immune system to attack the invader immediately should it ever recur. This is the body's natural way of fighting disease. Von Behring determined that animals with these antibodies to diphtheria toxins were immune to further infections of diphtheria. Their blood, injected into other animals, protected those animals from diphtheria infection, too. Von Behring began to use a herd of sheep to produce large quantities of the blood that fought off diphtheria. He used a purified mixture of this blood to develop an antitoxin serum to protect against diphtheria toxins. This blood serum therapy, as he called it, did not provide long-lasting protection as vaccines did, but amazingly it could be used as a treatment for animals already sickened with the bacteria that cause diphtheria. If it was given to them early in the course of the disease, it prevented the toxins from killing the animals.

Von Behring and other researchers from Koch's institute tried the antitoxin blood serum therapy on children hospitalized with diphtheria. It worked at least 75 percent of the time—saving many children who previously would have died. Diphtheria was a killer no more. In Germany alone, it was estimated that forty-five thousand children a year were saved with antitoxin therapy. Von Behring became known around the world as "the savior of the children."[25] He won the first ever Nobel Prize in Medicine in 1901. He is often considered the founder of immunology—the science of the immune system. Germ theory led von Behring to the study of how disease microbes behave, which led him to the discovery that blood forms antitoxins (or antibodies), which led to the first understanding of how the immune system combats disease.

Paul Ehrlich and his "Magic Bullet"

Still, diphtheria blood serum therapy was more like a weak vaccine than a treatment. It had to be given before the diphtheria microbes had begun to produce toxins in any quantity. Germ theory had helped

Ignaz Semmelweis, Promoter of Hand Washing

Long before Joseph Lister instituted antiseptic wound treatment, an obscure Hungarian-born physician named Ignaz Semmelweis discovered that simple hand washing by doctors drastically reduced the incidence of childbed fever in women giving birth. In 1847, in the Austrian hospital where he worked, Semmelweis ordered all his assistants to wash their hands thoroughly before they attended a woman in labor in the hospital. The incidence of childbed fever among women treated by Semmelweis and his assistants was almost immediately reduced from an average of 10 percent to just 1 or 2 percent.

Semmelweis's insistence that cleanliness would stop childbed fever was ridiculed and rejected by the other doctors at the hospital. He was labeled a troublemaker and fired. In his outrage, Semmelweis began writing angry letters to doctors throughout Europe, calling them murderers and trying to persuade them to believe him about hand washing. Everyone dismissed him. As the years passed he became more and more angry, moody, and unreasonable. His friends and family decided that he had lost his mind. (Historians today speculate that he may have been suffering from early dementia or a neurological disease.) Semmelweis was committed to a mental institution in 1865, where he was beaten to death by members of the staff. He was just forty-seven years old. Decades later, with germ theory firmly established, the medical world rediscovered Semmelweis and credited him with the recognition he deserved as a pioneer in infectious disease.

researchers understand microbes and gave rise to prevention methods and to vaccines, but finding true disease treatments and cures took longer. During the early 1900s almost no medicines or drugs existed that could make sick people well. The first actual chemical treatment for a disease was for the sexually transmitted disease syphilis. It was discovered by physician Paul Ehrlich. Ehrlich trained at Koch's laboratory in Berlin. He had been in the audience when Koch announced his discovery of the tuberculosis microbe to the Berlin Physiological Society. The memory of that event stayed with Ehrlich, who later

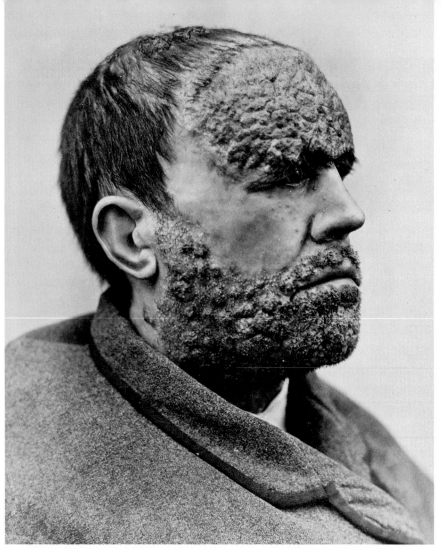

A colorized photograph from the 1860s shows large pus-filled eruptions on the face, neck, and head of a man who has an advanced case of syphilis. Physician Paul Ehrlich's efforts to help patients suffering from the disease led to the first treatment for a microbial illness.

said, "I hold that evening to be the most important experience of my scientific life."[26] When he got the chance to work with Koch in 1891, Ehrlich was thrilled. He assisted in the laboratory work with microbe identification and toxins and then became director of his own institute in Frankfort in 1899.

Ehrlich was an expert in the dyes and staining techniques that researchers used to study microbes. He was fascinated by the fact that different microbes and body tissues absorbed different kinds of dyes, and he developed the theory that a dye or chemical must exist that was absorbed by a particular kind of microbe but not by any body tissues or cells. Furthermore, such a chemical would harm or kill the microbe while leaving the body unharmed. Ehrlich explained,

> Curative substances—a priori—must directly destroy the microbes provoking the disease; not by an action from a distance but only when the chemical compound is fixed [absorbed] by the parasites. . . . This is a very difficult task because it is necessary to find chemical compounds, which have a strong destructive effect upon the parasites, but which do not at all, or only to a minimum extent, attack or damage the organs of the body.[27]

The chemical compounds would be the "magic bullets,"[28] he said, that could be shot at microbes and kill them. To prove his theory Ehrlich and his assistant, Sahachiro Hata, experimented with the corkscrew-shaped microbe that causes syphilis. Syphilis was a gruesome disease afflicting people in countries around the world. It was commonly called "the great pox" (to distinguish it from smallpox) and caused large pus-filled eruptions on the body, rashes, high fever, bone pain, and eventually nervous system damage that led to paralysis, insanity, and death.

At first with dyes and then with slightly different variations of arsenic-derived compounds, Ehrlich and Hata experimented with hundreds of different chemical substances on syphilis-infected laboratory rabbits. Finally in 1909, with compound number 606, they found their magic bullet. When Ehrlich gave this compound to a physician friend to try on his hospitalized patients, many of them were completely cured. Ehrlich named the compound Salvarsan, and by 1910 it was being sold throughout the world as a wonder drug. Ehrlich had developed the first treatment for a microbial disease, but he always gave the credit to Pasteur's formulation of germ theory and to Koch's proof of germ theory for making his research possible. Their work provided the basis for researchers' ability to cause infectious diseases in animals and then to grow pure cultures of specific bacteria from these animals. This ultimately enabled Ehrlich to experiment with ways to attack those microbes. Now, thought Ehrlich, the world had a way to develop chemical treatments and cures for many infectious diseases, but the next treatment breakthrough took much longer than Ehrlich expected. Chemical cures for diseases turned out to be very difficult to find.

The Discovery of Antibiotics

One of the first physicians in England to use Salvarsan for his syphilis patients was Alexander Fleming. By the 1900s all doctors, including Fleming, were believers in germ theory. Fleming served in military hospitals during World War I and was appalled by the number of infections soldiers suffered, even though all the doctors followed Lister's antiseptic standards. Infections deep inside wounds or in the bloodstream could not be addressed by sterilizing wounds. Recognizing that better treatments were needed, Fleming later wrote, "What we are looking for is some chemical substance which can be injected without danger into the bloodstream for the purpose of destroying the bacilli [bacteria] of infection, as Salvarsan destroys the spirochetes [corkscrew-shaped bacteria that cause syphilis]."[29]

After the war Fleming conducted laboratory research into antiseptic chemical compounds that could kill bacteria, but all his efforts failed until, in 1928, he carelessly left a petri dish of staph culture unprotected on a table. Fleming knew that cultures often became contaminated when exposed to the air, but this dish looked odd. A mold had contaminated the dish. All around the border of the mold almost none of the original staph bacteria were growing. They were dead. "That's funny,"[30] he remarked, and he immediately began investigating the mold. Perhaps it was the chemical substance—produced naturally by a living organism—that he had been searching for. He was not a chemist, so he asked a colleague to identify the strange mold. It was *Penicillium notatum*, and further research proved to Fleming that a substance secreted by this mold had unusual properties: it was a powerful killer of some kinds of bacteria. Fleming named the substance "penicillin" and tried to purify it, but it was so unstable that he failed in all his efforts to isolate it.

Almost no one in the scientific community was interested in Fleming's strange discovery, but he sent samples of the mold to various research institutes and laboratories, hoping to persuade someone

Saving Lives in India

Microbiologist Waldemar Haffkine was a Russian Jewish emigrant who came to work at the Pasteur Institute in 1888 because of prejudice in his home country. Pasteur welcomed him, and Haffkine developed the first cholera vaccine at Pasteur's laboratories. In 1893 Haffkine moved to India where hundreds of thousands of people died every year in infectious disease epidemics. In his first year there he vaccinated twenty-five thousand people against cholera. When Haffkine came down with malaria, he had to return to France to recover. In 1896 he went back to India and vaccinated another thirty thousand people in just seven months.

Then, an epidemic of bubonic plague struck. The Indian government was so impressed with Haffkine's success against cholera that officials begged him for help with the plague. By 1897 Haffkine had developed a plague vaccine. He publicly tested the first dose on himself to prove that it was safe. Then he tested it on some volunteer prisoners in a jail. When plague struck the jail, other inmates died but the vaccinated ones remained perfectly healthy. By 1900, 4 million people in India had been vaccinated against bubonic plague, and the epidemic was over. Haffkine was a hero in India, where he lived for much of the rest of his life and directed a research laboratory. His vaccines saved thousands of lives in countries around the world.

more skilled in biochemistry than he to identify and purify the substance the mold was producing. For nearly ten years he waited. Despite universal acceptance of germ theory, few scientists believed that chemical treatments for bacterial infections were practical. Then, in 1935, scientists at the Pasteur Institute discovered that a substance in a common dye, sulfanilamide, killed some bacteria. Sulfa drugs changed the attitude of medical researchers throughout the world, and they became seriously interested in finding other chemical agents that could fight harmful bacteria.

Even before germ theory scientists had known that some microorganisms have antibiotic (literally meaning "against life") properties against other microorganisms, but they did not think it was important until they understood that germs cause infections. In

1938, however, Howard Florey, Ernest Chain, and Norman Heatley at Oxford University read Fleming's research and discovered that they had an old sample of his penicillin mold stored at their university. Immediately the pathologist and two biochemists, who were researching antibacterial chemicals, recognized the possible importance of penicillin as a microbe killer and set to work to extract the tiny amounts of penicillin produced by the mold and then purify and

Alexander Fleming (pictured in his laboratory in 1951) uses a microscope to examine the contents of a petri dish. A laboratory accident involving a spoiled bacterial culture in a petri dish led to Fleming's discovery of the antibiotic properties of penicillin.

collect it. They tested the accumulated substance on mice infected by staph, strep, and other bacteria, and penicillin was monumentally successful. All the untreated mice died; all those treated were completely cured. Early testing on humans suggested good results, too, but the research team could not make enough penicillin to prove its worth conclusively. World War II was straining England's resources, so the team enlisted US production capabilities, and the wondrous miracle drug was manufactured in great quantity in America. Its effects on infections were amazing: penicillin cured. It seemed to science and the public the culmination of the blessings of germ theory. Humanity finally had the way to win the battle against microbes. Thousands of soldiers with gruesome battlefield wounds and infections were saved with penicillin, and the world no longer had to fear infections and many infectious diseases. During the 1940s other antibiotic discoveries from the natural, microscopic world quickly followed the discovery of penicillin, each with almost miraculous healing properties.

Pasteur Was Right

Fleming always remained humble about the lucky accident that led him to discover penicillin. He once explained, "Pasteur's often quoted dictum that Fortune favors the prepared mind is undoubtedly true, for the unprepared mind cannot see the outstretched hand of opportunity."[31] Fleming did see the opportunity in his contaminated petri dish, and as a result, he led germ theorists to new heights in the war against disease.

CHAPTER FOUR

Public Health

As germ theory took hold in medicine, it changed social perceptions and public attitudes toward diseases, infections, and the invisible world of microbes. Governments and populations embraced germ theory. Lifestyles, approaches to hygiene, and sanitation methods evolved, and the constant fearful threat of diseases and infections began to wane.

The Ease of Catching Tuberculosis

Once germ theory was established in the medical community, it quickly found its way into the consciousness of the public and radically changed the way that people viewed cleanliness and the dangers of contagious diseases. An 1885 article in the magazine *Popular Science Monthly*, for example, explains, "The germ theory appeals to the average mind: it is something tangible; it may be hunted down, captured, cultured, and looked at through a microscope, and then in all its varieties, it can be held directly responsible for so much damage."[32] At first, the awareness of germs affected mostly wealthy and prosperous middle class people, but eventually it found its way into all classes of society. Perhaps nowhere did germ theory affect attitudes and behaviors as much as it did with the 1882 announcement by Robert Koch that tuberculosis was caused by a microbe and was a contagious disease that could be passed from person to person.

At the time Koch made the discovery of the tuberculosis bacterium, TB could affect any organ in the body, but 75 percent of the time it attacked the lungs. The common name for this form of the disease was "consumption" because people seemed consumed by it. As TB progressed, people seemed to waste away from exhaustion and weakness. And, as breathing became more and more difficult, they began coughing up blood and sputum (spit and phlegm). No one suspected that they had caught the disease from the coughs and sputum of someone with active TB. Normal cultural practices of the time aided TB's spread. For example, people spit wherever and whenever they felt like it, in public or at home. People thought nothing of sharing drinking cups and eating utensils, or even—in the case of babies—chewing food and passing it from mouth to mouth. Families shared toothbrushes. In hotels people shared beds with strangers, sick or well. In private homes family members cared for TB victims in hot rooms with tightly closed windows and doors, which was supposed to protect the patients from harmful fresh air. In sum, no one thought about contamination or contagion, and therefore, especially in cities, infectious diseases spread rampantly. In Europe the incidence of mortality from TB was 500 out of every 100,000 people. In the United States, as late as 1905, tuberculosis killed 180 out of every 100,000 people. It was the leading cause of death, outranking cancer, accidents, heart disease, influenza, and pneumonia.

Spitting and Coughing

Germ theory gave populations and governments a new way to avoid or prevent TB infections by controlling the means of contagion. Popular magazines, newspapers, medical speakers, and books preached the dangers of germs to the public. Public health departments and private associations and charities instituted anti-tuberculosis educational campaigns that taught how TB is spread, how to avoid infecting others, and how to protect oneself from TB germs. In their zeal, these groups often exaggerated the hygiene methods necessary to avoid germs, but they used the best information available at the time and succeeded in persuading a whole generation to change its ways and learn to fear germs.

Anti-spitting campaigns had major success. Public Health departments passed laws against spitting in public and persuaded bars, stores, hotels, and other businesses to get rid of the spittoons that were always available for men chewing tobacco to spit into. Spitting on sidewalks came to be seen as disgusting and a peril to society. Concerned health workers and doctors established the National Tuberculosis Association (NTA), which also began selling Christmas Seals. The NTA as well as other volunteer health organizations launched programs to educate the public about the dangers of spitting. The NTA distributed a pamphlet that explains about TB victims, "The germ, which is a microscopic rod, is found in millions in their spit from very early in the disease, and it is through this spit alone that it reaches others." They came up with slogans such as "Spitting is dangerous, indecent and against the law" and "No spit, no consumption."[33]

People with consumption were urged in every way possible to protect their families and other citizens from catching TB. In 1910 Thomas Edison produced a series of public health movies for the NTA that taught the "careless consumptive"[34] how to prevent giving TB to others. Among other advice, the movies taught that people should cover their mouths when they coughed, keep their rooms ventilated so that germs in the air would not infect others, practice careful cleanliness in their homes, and wash their hands frequently to get rid of TB germs. Movies, posters, pamphlets, and educational lectures impressed citizens with the reality of TB germs and often scared them into changing their lifestyle habits.

New Cleanliness Standards

Even dust and clothing became targets of a cleanliness crusade. Women were convinced that how well they cleaned their houses would determine whether their families contracted TB. Most scientists of the time believed and taught that tuberculosis bacteria were much more long-lived than they actually are. They thought that TB germs could float in the air, settle on dust motes, and drift into corners or under furniture where they remained alive for weeks and could infect people. The experts were also convinced that the germs lived on public streets where people had spit and could be carried home on the hems of women's long skirts that dragged on the ground in the dust. Once inside the home, these bacteria could sicken household members. One American bacteriologist, T. Mitchell Prudden, who trained at Koch's institute, argued, "The reason why consumption is so widespread . . . is simply that consumptive persons, either from ignorance or carelessness, are distributing the poison not only everywhere they go, but everywhere the dust goes which has been formed in part by the undestroyed germ-laden material expelled from their lungs."[35]

None of this was true, but germ theory soon gave rise to a cleanliness mania, first in wealthy and middle-class homes and then even in the rural, poor, and immigrant segments of society. Housewives and domestic servants worked hard to eliminate the dust hiding in their homes. Newly invented vacuum cleaners became extremely popular as the way to remove dangerous dust instead of stirring it up by sweeping. Women's dress fashions changed, and shorter, ankle-length skirts that did not drag in the dust became the norm. Since unsuspected germs

A health department sign from an earlier era warns pedestrians to avoid spitting on sidewalks. Signs such as these appeared worldwide in the early 1900s as health departments struggled to contain the highly contagious disease tuberculosis.

The First Public Health Nurse

In 1893 Lillian Wald founded the first visiting nurse service in New York City to help the poor immigrant populations in the city's tenements to improve their health, learn cleanliness standards, and reduce their incidence of infectious diseases. First with private financial backing and then with government funds, she organized a group of nurses to provide preventive care and improved health for thousands of people then living in squalor. Wald named these workers "public health nurses." The nurses offered free treatment to sick people, threatened tenement owners and supervisors into cleaning up rat-infested buildings and repairing nonfunctional plumbing, and educated TB victims and their families about how to prevent contagion. The nurses went into the schools and identified children with infections such as scarlet fever, quarantined them from the classroom until they were well, and educated teachers about how to recognize contagious diseases. They instituted a school nursing program that was eventually imitated nationwide.

As germ theory gained acceptance, Wald's efforts to reform the living conditions of the poor and to bring infectious disease control efforts to schools were embraced by society. State funding of public health nursing and school nurse programs became the norm throughout the United States.

could be present in any stranger, hotels began to provide clean sheets to cover blankets and to change them with every new customer. Schools eliminated the common drinking cup or water dipper with bucket and installed water fountains or offered paper cups to the students. School teachers educated children to wash their hands before every meal and to cover their noses and mouths when they sneezed or coughed. Churches stopped the practice of including a common communion cup in their services. Parents were urged not to let strangers kiss their babies. Even men's whiskers and beards came under attack as a dirty site where germs could lie hidden. One slogan urged, "Sacrifice Whiskers and Save Children,"[36] and clean-shaven faces became the new normal.

The complete acceptance of the existence of germs and consequent public efforts to avoid germs did help reduce the incidence of TB. Along with cleanliness and behaviors to avoid contagion, the sanatorium movement, which isolated TB patients in care facilities for treatment, dramatically slowed the infection rates for TB. As more and more patients were effectively quarantined, TB ceased to be the major public health threat it had been before germ theory.

Learning the Dangers of Human Wastes

Tuberculosis was not the only disease that imperiled people in the early twentieth century, nor was it the only disease subjected to public health interventions. In 1892 a cholera epidemic struck Hamburg, Germany; seventeen thousand people were infected with the severe diarrheal disease, and eight thousand died. Koch traveled to the city and proved that cholera bacteria from raw sewage that contaminated the city's water supply were responsible. He also demonstrated that water filtration systems successfully kept all kinds of bacteria out of drinking water. Cities throughout Europe and America learned the way to prevent such diseases as cholera and typhoid (another diarrheal disease) that were spread through infected human feces that contaminated water. Medical professor Robert P. Gaynes says, "Water filtration plants in cities throughout the world owe a great debt to Robert Koch."[37]

Understanding that germs cause disease logically led researchers to explore and determine all the ways in which infecting germs were transmitted. Infections did not always pass directly from person to person. Some were transmitted in water and others by insects, particularly flies. Flies, for example, could walk through and feed on exposed, disease-carrying human feces and then walk on the food and water people ingested, thereby providing another way that diseases such as cholera, typhoid, and dysentery were transmitted. Both human wastes and common house flies became the targets of public health campaigns and public prevention efforts. Outdoor toilets were enclosed, and in cities sewage treatment plants were established. Window screens became popular and common in private homes as the way to exclude disease-carrying flies from the environment. Luxurious bathrooms with their old-fashioned wooden toilets, carpeting,

German soldiers on the Eastern Front during World War I get drinking water after it has been run through a filtration system. Water filtration systems were used to eliminate disease-causing bacteria and thus prevent illnesses that spread through contaminated water.

and draperies disappeared. Instead, people installed porcelain enameled toilets surrounded by tiles—all slick surfaces that were easy to clean and could not hide germs. Public Health departments and private educational associations launched crusades against flies with fear tactics that emphasized the risk of disease. One 1917 poster warns, "Death Lurks in the Filth on a Fly's Feet!," and another cautions, "Don't Let That Fly Become a Grandfather. KILL IT NOW!"[38]

Mosquito-Borne Diseases

The discovery that the disease germs that cause yellow fever and malaria were carried by mosquitoes also changed public health around the world. Yellow fever is characterized by a yellowing skin, headaches, high fevers, and black vomit. It killed as many as 50 percent of people who contracted it. People with malaria suffer repeated bouts of fever, sweating, chills, nausea, vomiting, and anemia. Malaria can kill many of its victims, especially children and those who are already old or vulnerable because of other health problems. Although most commonly diseases of the tropics, both malaria and yellow fever occurred in the United States into the twentieth century. Epidemics of the diseases waned only with the first frosts of autumn.

In Cuba in 1900, where many American soldiers were threatened by yellow fever, Walter Reed, an army physician inspired by germ theory, proved that bites from infected mosquitoes were the sole cause of yellow fever, even though the disease germ is a virus that was too small to be seen. Reed conducted a series of experiments with volunteers who allowed mosquitoes that had fed off yellow fever patients to bite them. In one of the experiments Reed built a small house with a floor-to-ceiling fine mesh wire screen dividing the house in half. On one side a volunteer lived with fifteen mosquitoes that had fed on yellow fever patients. On the other side volunteers stayed for eighteen days, protected from the mosquitoes but living with the clothes and bed sheets of yellow fever patients. All of the latter remained healthy behind the screen, but the man who lived with the mosquitoes almost died of the fever. Now Reed was positive that mosquitoes carried the yellow fever germ from person to person. That was why epidemics occurred. Reed instituted programs of mosquito control, such as screening all living quarters and draining water ditches, and yellow fever disappeared.

Major Ronald Ross, a British physician, found the microscopic parasite that causes malaria in the stomach of an infected mosquito in 1897. By 1904, during the building of the Panama Canal, the same mosquito control efforts that had been used against yellow fever were used to control malaria among American construction workers. Fine mesh screens were installed in doors and windows of all homes. Pools, ditches, and cisterns—where mosquitoes could breed—were drained. Ponds and swamps were treated with layers of oil so that mosquitoes could not breed, and a primitive kind of insecticide was developed using carbolic acid to kill mosquito larvae. Brush and tall grasses where mosquitoes could hide were cut short. People were even hired to kill adult mosquitoes hiding in tents, buildings, and homes. Mosquito control efforts were remarkably successful in ending the threat of yellow fever and malaria epidemics. In both Cuba and Panama yellow fever was eradicated, and malaria cases were drastically reduced.

The lessons learned overseas quickly translated into public health measures in the United States. The public learned to use fine mesh, metal screens on all doors and windows and to eliminate any open cisterns, rain barrels, or pools of standing water around their homes. States formed mosquito control associations that worked to eradicate mosquitoes through drainage and insecticidal efforts. As a direct result of these programs, the last yellow fever epidemic in the United States occurred in 1905. Paul de Kruif says of this consequence of the application of germ theory, "It vindicates Pasteur!"[39]

Vaccines and Public Health

Pasteur's development of a vaccination method to protect humanity from microbes confirms the tremendous value of germ theory, as well. Vaccines are all made in a similar way and have a similar action: weakened or killed microbes for a specific disease are injected into a person in order to stimulate antibody production and provide immunity to that disease. One by one, deadly diseases were defanged during the 1930s as vaccination programs eliminated disease threats in developed countries. Whooping cough, diphtheria, tetanus, bubonic plague, yellow fever, typhoid, and cholera were just some of the frightening diseases that became preventable with new vaccines.

Death rates from these diseases plummeted, especially among children as parents flocked to obtain vaccinations for their families. State Public Health departments passed regulations requiring childhood vaccinations before school entrance, and these widespread vaccination efforts changed families' lives. People no longer lived with the anxiety and fear that their loved ones could be taken from them at any time. They were no longer helpless against the diseases that had regularly killed their children and made every parent unsure whether a child would successfully reach adulthood. Before the diphtheria vaccine, for example, the United States had about thirty thousand cases of diphtheria each year, with three thousand deaths. After the vaccine, diphtheria became almost unknown in both Europe and America. The Centers for Disease Control and Prevention (CDC) says today, "Vaccines are one of the greatest achievements of biomedical science and public health."[40] *New York Times* writer Donald G. McNeil Jr. notes, "In addition, vaccination is one of the leading reasons that many families in the West now feel comfortable having only two or three children: they can be reasonably certain that the children will survive childhood."[41]

How Vaccines Work

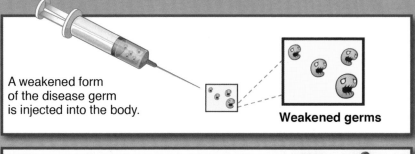

A weakened form of the disease germ is injected into the body.

Weakened germs

The body makes antibodies to fight these invaders.

Antibodies

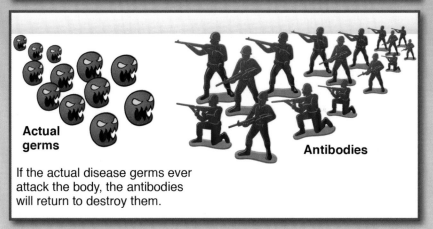

Actual germs

Antibodies

If the actual disease germs ever attack the body, the antibodies will return to destroy them.

Source: Centers for Disease Control and Prevention, "Why Are Childhood Vaccines So Important?" www.cdc.gov.

The War Against Germs Seems Won

After antibiotics were developed during the decades of the 1940s, 1950s, and 1960s, germ theory seemed to have given humanity all that was necessary to win the battle against germs. Antibiotics cured bacterial infections. New vaccines ended the threat of diseases such as polio, measles, mumps, and rubella (also known as German measles).

Deadly Food

Before germ theory, contaminated food often sickened and killed. Historian Nancy Tomes says, "Given how hard it is to prevent food poisoning even today, we can hardly begin to imagine how frequently Americans suffered from foodborne disease in the nineteenth century." People routinely left cooked food sitting on the table for hours before a meal. Pantry foods were commonly walked on by insects and rodents. Home canning was often done at unsafe low temperatures. Grocers sold bread unwrapped and casually left it on open counters. They did the same with fruits and vegetables. Dairymen distributed milk to their customers by ladling it from open pails that were often contaminated by dirt and manure from barns.

In 1888 German scientist August Gartner discovered the bacterium now known as *Salmonella enteritidis* in spoiled meat. In 1895 Belgian scientist Émile-Pierre-Marie Van Ermengem isolated the often fatal microbe that causes botulism poisoning and infects poorly canned foods. As people learned about diseases caused by lack of food safety, everything changed. Milk was sold in sterilized and sealed glass bottles. Grocery stores sold foods guaranteed pure, safe, and hygienically packaged. Families learned sterile methods of food preservation and safety methods for storing and protecting foods. Tomes says that, in essence, the public and businesses accepted "laboratory-inspired disciplines designed to safeguard the food supply against dangerous microorganisms." And thousands of lives were saved.

Nancy Tomes, *The Gospel of Germs: Men, Women, and the Microbe in American Life.* Cambridge, MA: Harvard University Press, 1998, pp. 5, 102–103.

Quite quickly, people forgot their fears of diseases and epidemics and thought of the dangers as a thing of the past. Both the public and the medical profession became complacent about germs and infections. Gaynes explains, "I entered the specialty at a time [1978] when it was believed that medical science had nearly done it all—that there would be little left to do since we had such powerful agents for treating and curing infectious diseases."[42] The heirs of germ theory thought that microbes had been finally conquered.

CHAPTER FIVE

The Unconquered

Germ theory has provided tools for preventing, treating, and curing sickness, but microbes are far from conquered. The success of germ theory produced not an end to infectious disease but—at least in part—a forgetfulness of its dangers. In addition, microbes have remarkable strategies for survival that early germ theorists never suspected.

Believing in the Dangers of Germs

Early germ theorists were intensely aware of microbial threats. Pasteur, for example, was seriously vigilant about germs and scrupulously clean in his personal life. He could not forget that dangerous, invisible microbes were everywhere. In an early biography of Pasteur, his son-in-law, Rene Vallery-Radot reports:

> He never used a plate or a glass without examining them minutely and wiping them carefully; no microscopic speck of dust escaped his short-sighted eyes. Whether at home or with strangers he invariably went through this preliminary exercise, in spite of the anxious astonishment of his hostess, who usually feared that some negligence had occurred, until Pasteur, noticing her slight dismay, assured her that this was but the inveterate scientist's habit.[43]

Later, with Joseph Lister's dire warnings about the dangers of microbes, the medical community became painstakingly vigilant about microbial threats. Doctors and nurses emphasized hand washing, clean uniforms, sterile gloves, and eliminating germs from the environment in surgery, obstetrics, and general hospital care. Hospital infections plummeted because of these widespread efforts to adhere to germ theory principles. Modern physician Miguel A. Faria Jr. explains: "The period between 1930 and 1940 saw a sharply rising curve in longevity rates thanks to the widespread usage of antibiotics and the much improved standards in cleanliness, hygiene, and sanitation. Thereafter, further reductions in maternal and infant mortalities were to a significant degree responsible for the tremendous rise in life expectancy."[44]

Getting Complacent About Germs

Germ theory led to longer, healthier lives for people in developed countries, but modern medicine often forgets the lessons of the past. Health care workers have become less careful and scrupulous about eliminating germs and infections. Cleanliness standards have dropped. Today in the US alone, some eighty thousand people die of health care–related infections each year. Public health expert Elizabeth Pfoh, physician Sydney Dy, and professor Cyrus Engineer say in a 2013 report, "Yet these infections are frequently preventable through hand hygiene."[45] The researchers explain that the problem is not that health care workers do not believe in germ theory. The problem is that they often underestimate the importance of hand washing and disinfecting and overestimate how often they do it. As in times past, modern doctors and nurses sometimes assume they are clean because their hands *look* clean or they tire of having to constantly disinfect their hands.

In a recent study physician Jonathan D. Katz reports that on average, health care workers wash their hands only about 48 percent of the time, and physicians (other than surgeons) are worse than nurses. Katz also found that health care workers who do wash their hands often do not do a thorough job of it; instead of scrubbing the recommended thirty seconds, they average about ten seconds. Lax hand washing practices are largely to blame for the spread of infection in hospitals. Katz says, "The majority of these infections are caused by the

Surgeons wash their hands before entering an operating room. Hand-washing and other measures have become standard practice for cleanliness in hospitals, but recent studies show less vigilance in this area among contemporary health care workers.

transmission of microorganisms on the hands of health care providers who have either not washed their hands or did so inadequately between patients."[46] Modern hospitals are failing to protect people from hospital-caused infections as they neglect the fundamental teachings of germ theory.

Antibiotic Resistance

The development of antibiotics, once viewed as the ultimate triumph over germs, has introduced a new and troubling problem. While antibiotics represent a truly important treatment for many infections, their overuse has helped some microbes survive. "In the 1950s," says Robert P. Gaynes,

the use and overuse of penicillin resulted in penicillin resistance. In the 1960s and 1970s, the use and overuse of streptomycin resulted in streptomycin resistance. With each new class of antibiotics, the observation that resistance follows use has been repeatedly made. Because antibiotics are typically well tolerated and effective, they are often used when the diagnosis of a bacterial infection is unclear. This liberal use of antibiotics has contributed to antibiotic resistance—a problem that has become a crisis.[47]

The more frequently microbes are exposed to antibiotics, the more likely the bacteria become able to fight back. When bacteria are exposed to the appropriate antibiotic, most are killed, but a few—those with a slightly different genetic structure—survive. They are the ones that live to multiply and to be able to resist that antibiotic. This is how MRSA (methicillin-resistant *Staphylococcus aureus*) arose during the 1960s. It is the staph germ that has developed a resistance to the penicillin-like antibiotic that was most effective against it. MRSA has become a serious and leading cause of hospital infections that can be difficult to treat and lead to death when the germ invades the lungs or the bloodstream. Few antibiotics are effective against MRSA, and as the bacterium continues to evolve through slight genetic changes, or mutations, many scientists fear that MRSA may someday be resistant to all known antibiotics.

The same resistance problem has developed with the bacteria that cause tuberculosis, which is still a common disease in the developing world. In 1943 Albert Schatz and Selman Waksman discovered streptomycin, an antibiotic that cures tuberculosis. More and more powerful antibiotics that killed TB bacteria soon followed. Since that time, however, mostly because of overuse and misuse of the drug (such as taking the wrong dose), TB bacteria have become resistant to the drugs most effective against the disease. Multidrug-resistant tuberculosis has become a major public health problem around the world and is extremely difficult to treat. The wonder drugs that are antibiotics have not conquered the microbial world after all, as the early germ theorists believed that they would.

A New Understanding of Ulcers and Stomach Cancer

Germ theory has not solved every infectious disease problem, but it continues to be the pathway to identifying previously unknown microbes and tackling threatening diseases. In 1981, for example, Australian physician Barry Marshall became convinced that gastritis (inflammation of the stomach), ulcers (open sores in the stomach or intestine), and stomach cancer are caused by a microbe. A colleague, pathologist Robin Warren, had found previously unknown corkscrew-shaped bacteria in the stomachs of some hospital patients, and this discovery piqued Marshall's interest. In his laboratory Marshall examined samples taken from his ulcer and stomach cancer patients and found heavy infestations of the strange bacteria, later named *Helicobacter pylori* (*H. pylori*). Marshall believed that

The bacteria known as MRSA can be seen in this scanning electron micrograph. A leading cause of infections in hospitals, MRSA is antibiotic-resistant and therefore difficult to treat.

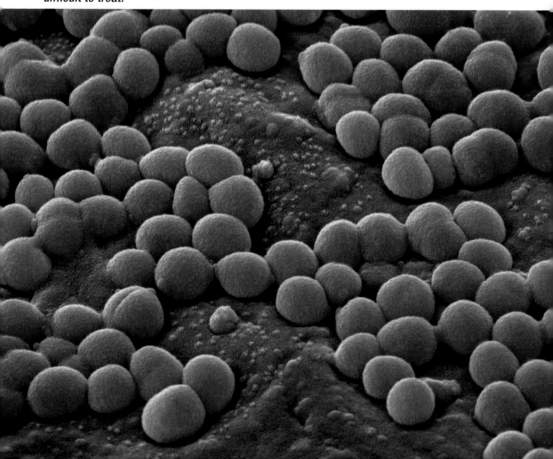

The Business of Germ Theory

In 1876 a young American businessman named Robert Wood Johnson attended a speech on antisepsis given by Joseph Lister. Johnson was so inspired that he founded a company with his two brothers in 1886 to manufacture sterile bandages, surgical thread, surgical gauze, and surgical dressings so that doctors no longer had to make their own. In 1888 that company, Johnson & Johnson, published a small book titled *Modern Methods of Antiseptic Wound Treatment* that became a teaching tool for practicing sterile surgery around the world. Lister himself wrote to Johnson & Johnson to inquire about their sterile methods of laboratory manufacture and praise the company's efforts. The company went on to produce first aid kits, baby powder, dental floss, and bandages. The company also sells Listerine mouthwash, named for Joseph Lister. It was originally developed by a Missouri doctor in 1879 as a surgical antiseptic. By 1914 Listerine was sold as an oral antiseptic and mouthwash to the general public. In 2006 Johnson & Johnson bought the company that owned the mouthwash, and Listerine became Johnson & Johnson's oldest product still being sold today.

these bacteria were the cause of gastritis, which led to ulcers and stomach cancer. If true, this would topple the long-held view that ulcers were caused by stress—and few in the medical community saw merit in Marshall's theory.

To prove his theory Marshall turned to germ theory and Koch's postulates. Marshall took stomach tissue samples from many ulcer and cancer patients and always found the bacteria when inflammation was present. He succeeded in growing pure cultures of *H. pylori* in his lab. He even determined which antibiotic could kill the bacteria. However, he could not then inject the cultures into lab animals to see if they developed the disease because *H. pylori* afflicts only humans and some other primates. So Marshall decided to test his theory on himself. He made a pure *H. pylori* broth and drank it. Five days later, Marshall developed gastritis. He started vomiting and then developed an ulcer. After ten days he had an endoscopy—a medical examination of his stomach through a tube that also snipped out a tissue sample. His stomach was inflamed and teeming with *Helicobacter pylori*.

Just as Robert Koch had done with the TB bacterium, Marshall had proved that stomach inflammation was caused by *H. pylori*, but the medical world was slow to accept his findings. Marshall says, "You think, 'It's science; it's got to be accepted.' But it's not an absolute given. The idea was too weird."[48] Marshall had as many doubters as Louis Pasteur had when he first proposed germ theory. Over the next ten years, as Marshall cured his own ulcer and gastritis patients, doctors gradually came to realize that Marshall had to be right. In 2005 Marshall and Warren won a Nobel Prize for their discovery. And as gastritis and ulcers were routinely healed with antibiotics throughout the developed world, stomach cancer ceased developing in inflamed stomachs as well. Stomach cancer used to be one of the most common forms of cancer in the Western world. Today it has been almost completely eliminated, thanks to Marshall and germ theory.

The Challenge of Ebola

Marshall employed germ theory to identify a disease-causing microbe and then determine a treatment for it. Standard germ theory techniques for determining how a disease is transmitted and how to prevent or avoid epidemics when treatments or vaccines are unavailable continue to be an essential part of modern medicine, as well. The Ebola virus, for example, is one of a family of viruses that cause hemorrhagic fevers— a group of serious diseases characterized by bleeding in the internal organs. The viruses affect multiple body systems, including the blood vessels, the body's ability to regulate temperature, the immune system, and the kidneys. Ebola is an especially severe and deadly hemorrhagic fever that kills an average of 70 percent of victims. The disease and

the virus that causes it were discovered in 1976 in the Democratic Republic of Congo, near the Ebola River for which it is named. Since its discovery periodic small outbreaks of the disease have occurred in

Africa, but in 2014 an Ebola outbreak developed into a true epidemic. Medical researchers have been challenged to understand Ebola's transmission, contain the epidemic, and search for an effective means of prevention. Germ theory principles that evolved during the nineteenth and twentieth centuries are as relevant today as they were for past yellow fever, smallpox, and tuberculosis epidemics.

Like yellow fever, which is carried by mosquitoes, Ebola is also carried by animals. Ebola transmission, however, seems to be more complex than that of yellow fever. Scientists are still not sure what animal transmits Ebola, but they believe that fruit bats carry the virus without being sickened by it. Then, fruit bats are eaten by humans and nonhuman primates, or fruit bat droppings contaminate fruits eaten by primates and sicken them, and then the diseased animals are eaten by people. In this way, scientists theorize, the virus is first transmitted to a human being. Like plague, Ebola is then also passed from person to person. The bodily fluids of people sick with Ebola—such as blood, vomit, feces, and saliva—are teeming with contagious Ebola viruses. Anyone who comes into contact with the fluids is at risk for catching the disease and spreading it further.

Preventing Ebola by eliminating the carrier (as yellow fever was stopped by eliminating mosquitoes) is not an option. No one wants to exterminate bats or primates, even if that were possible in the vast wild forests of Africa. Preventing person-to-person transmission, however, through education, quarantine, and avoiding contact with bodily fluids can reduce infections and epidemics just as those methods worked with tuberculosis. Health care workers in Africa and treatment facilities in the developed world avoid contagion by placing patients in quarantine and wearing special protective clothing that prevents contact with bodily fluids. They sterilize and disinfect this protective gear, any patient bedding and clothing that may harbor fluids, and all medical instruments and equipment used to treat the Ebola patient. They also often place themselves in quarantine if they fear that they have been exposed to the virus so as not to further its spread. These measures are not always effective at preventing transmission. One slight mistake involving skin exposure to fluids can lead to transmission of the virus to an individual. However, the chance of an outbreak or epidemic is eliminated by strict adherence to germ theory infection prevention methods.

Too Worried About Germs?

The hygiene standards in hospitals may be too lax, but many scientists worry that the general public is overdoing its war on germs. Antibiotic, antimicrobial, and antiseptic household consumer products are everywhere. The public can buy and use antibacterial soaps, deodorants, dish cleaning liquids, detergents, and sanitizing wipes, among other hygiene products. One study found that the products are in 75 percent of American homes. In a large study from Columbia University, Elaine Larson and her scientific team examined hand washing in healthy people. The study found no difference in sanitation or health between people who wash their hands with regular soaps and those who use antibacterial soaps.

Many scientists also think that antibacterial products may do more harm than good. They can kill the beneficial bacteria on human skin, thereby allowing harmful bacteria a place to grow. When they go down household drains, into city water supplies, they may kill weak, relatively harmless bacteria while letting stronger, more dangerous bacteria survive. In the home, these sanitizing products may be helping multiantibiotic-resistant bacteria to develop and multiply. Finally, some scientists theorize that humans must be exposed to some harmful bacteria to help the immune system to function correctly. Perhaps, they say, problems such as asthma and allergies are caused by the modern obsession with cleanliness. The US Centers for Disease Control and Prevention (CDC) warns that overuse of antimicrobial household products may be dangerous, both for people and for the environment.

Ongoing Suspicion and Disbelief

Ebola health care workers also attempt to educate the public, especially in West Africa, about how the disease is spread and how to avoid infection. Germ theory, however, is a product of Western medicine that is either unknown or not accepted in many parts of Africa. Millions of people believe that Ebola and other diseases are caused by curses, evil spirits, sickening vapors in the environment, or a punishment from God. The idea of unseen germs makes no sense to them. In these cultures, persuading people to wash their hands or isolate themselves when they are sick or avoid contact with the bodily fluids of their loved ones and neighbors is extremely difficult. Some people in Africa even believe that health care workers, in their strange protective gear, are trying to sicken and kill them or at least steal Ebola victims from their families. In parts of West Africa, the Ebola epidemic spreads unabated. Otula Owuor, the editor of the publication *ScienceAfrica*, laments that his continent "is still overwhelmed with myths, superstition especially the widespread horrifying lack of germ theory of diseases among the public."[49]

Even in the Western world, however, where germ theory is a mainstay of medical science, small segments of the public deny the reality of germ theory. Shawn Sieracki, for example, is a practitioner of alternative medicine who believes that diseases can be treated naturally and without the use of drugs or surgery. He rejects germ theory by saying, "It's not the germs that cause the disease. It's the condition of the environment that causes the disease."[50] In other words, the germs are there because the disease is there, not because they caused the dis-

A Red Cross team at an Ebola treatment center in Liberia in 2014 wears full protective gear. The highly contagious disease has killed thousands of people in Africa, including many health workers.

ease. Sieracki and other germ theory deniers argue that a naturally healthy body, fed by proper nutrition, is not susceptible to sickness and therefore does not invite any germs into its environment. Some also argue that the germs in a diseased body are actually acting to heal the disease and help the body to get rid of it, just as scavengers clean up Earth's environment and help it stay healthy.

In Europe and North America, the anti-vaccine movement represents another rejection of germ theory principles. Sometimes, anti-vaccine proponents believe that vaccinations cause other diseases. For instance, although numerous scientific studies have disproved the connection, many people believe vaccines cause autism. Other times, people worry that vaccines are not safe, cause serious side effects, or are just unnecessary in the modern world in which vaccine-preventable diseases are rare. As vaccination rates have dropped because of these concerns, outbreaks of preventable diseases, such as mumps, whooping cough, and measles have increased.

WORDS IN CONTEXT

alternative medicine
Various methods of treating and preventing disease, such as herbal treatments, homeopathy, or acupuncture, that are not included in traditional Western medical education and practice.

Firmly Founded on Germ Theory to Save Lives

Even as small segments of modern society reject the value of vaccines, medical researchers continue to focus on developing new vaccines to fight the diseases for which no treatment or cure yet exists. Researchers, for instance, are rushing to develop an Ebola vaccine that can stop the epidemic in West Africa. The World Health Organization (WHO) hopes that at least one will be ready for use sometime in 2015. If any of these experimental Ebola vaccines work, they may represent the world's one true opportunity to end another fearsome and dangerous disease.

In the meantime, doctors caring for Ebola victims have looked to the past for ways to treat the disease. Much like Emil von Behring's blood serum therapy to treat diphtheria in the 1880s, some doctors are creating a serum from the blood of individuals who have survived an Ebola infection. When the serum is injected into a sick patient, the patient receives antibodies to fight the disease. This approach seems to have worked in some, though not all, cases.

Medical scientists of today still believe that germ theory holds the ultimate answer to eradicating disease. Infectious disease specialist Philip S. Brachman warns, however, that "our infectious disease guard cannot be reduced. We are making progress in controlling and preventing infectious diseases but we must not become complacent."[51] New and reemerging disease threats require new research and new control and prevention methods so that the promise of germ theory will reach fruition.

SOURCE NOTES

Introduction: Transforming Medicine and the World

1. Quoted in "The Death of President Garfield, 1881," EyeWitness to History, 1999. eyewitnesstohistory.com.
2. Benjamin L. Aaron and S. David Rockoff, "The Attempted Assassination of President Reagan: Medical Implications and Historical Perspective," abstract, *JAMA*, vol. 272, no. 21, December 7, 1994. http://jama.jamanetwork.com.

Chapter One: Before Germ Theory

3. Quoted in Mary Lewise Barry Todd, "The Quest of the Individual: Interpreting the Narrative Structure in the Miracle Windows at Canterbury Cathedral," *Electronic Theses, Treatises and Dissertations*, paper 1290, Florida State University, July 11, 2007, p. 12. http://diginole.lib.fsu.edu.
4. Quoted in History Learning Site, "Ancient Egyptian Medicine," 2005. www.historylearningsite.co.uk.
5. Avicenna, "Thesis V. The Changes in the Atmosphere," *Canon of Medicine*, Part III, reprint, Canon of Medicine.com, pp. 2012–14. www.canonofmedicine.com.
6. Quoted in "Black Death: Facts and Summary," History. www.history.com.
7. Quoted in M. Iqtedar Husain Farooqi, "Medicine of the Prophet (Tibb al-Nabvi)," Islamic Research Foundation International. www.irfi.org.
8. Brought to Life: Science Museum.org, "Miasma Theory," Science Museum, London. www.sciencemuseum.org.uk.
9. Quoted in Carl S. Sterner, "A Brief History of Miasmic Theory," 2007, p. 3. www.carlsterner.com.
10. Quoted in Sheryl Persson, *Smallpox, Syphilis and Salvation: Medical Breakthroughs That Changed the World*. Auckland, NZ: Exisle, 2010, p. 12.
11. Quoted in Johanna Laybourn-Parry, *A Functional Biology of Free-Living Protozoa*. Berkeley: University of California Press, 1984, p. 111.

12. Quoted in University of California Museum of Paleontology, "Antony van Leeuwenhoek (1632–1723)." www.ucmp.berkeley.edu.

13. Quoted in Paul de Kruif, *Microbe Hunters*. New York: Houghton Mifflin Harcourt, 1926, p. 9.

Chapter Two: The Celebrated Founders of Germ Theory

14. Quoted in Michael Berger, Oliver Muensterer, and Carroll M. Harmon, "Tales from Previous Times: Important Eponyms in Pediatric Surgery," author's personal copy, *Pediatric Surgery International,* Springer-Verlag Berlin Heidelberg 2013, July 23, 2013, p. 2. www.researchgate.net.

15. Quoted in De Kruif, *Microbe Hunters*, p. 56.

16. De Kruif, *Microbe Hunters*, pp. 64–65.

17. Quoted in De Kruif, *Microbe Hunters*, pp. 81–82.

18. Quoted in Mary Bagley, "Louis Pasteur: Biography and Quotes," LiveScience, January 31, 2014. www.livescience.com.

19. Quoted in College of Physicians of Philadelphia, "Koch's Postulates," The History of Vaccines. www.historyofvaccines.org.

20. Quoted in W.F. Bynum, *Science and the Practice of Medicine in the Nineteenth Century*. New York: Cambridge University Press, 1994, p. 131.

21. Quoted in William John Bishop, *The Early History of Surgery*. New York: Barnes & Noble, 1995, p. 167.

22. Quoted in William Watson Cheyne, *Lister and His Achievement*. London: Longman's, Green and Co., 1925, p. 50. http://archive.org.

23. Quoted in J.D. Weis, "Pasteur—His Work and What It Has Done for Medicine," in *New Orleans Medical and Surgical Journal*, vol. 75, Louisiana State Medical Society. New Orleans: Andree Printery, 1922–1923, p. 508. http://books.google.com.

Chapter Three: The Revolution in Medicine

24. Quoted in De Kruif, *Microbe Hunters*, p. 133.

25. Quoted in Humboldt-Universität Zu Berlin, Nobel Prize Winners, "Emil von Behring," 2011. www.hu-berlin.de.

26. Quoted in Robert P. Gaynes, *Germ Theory: Medical Pioneers in Infectious Diseases*, Kindle edition. Washington, DC: ASM, 2011.

27. Quoted in Gaynes, *Germ Theory*.

28. Quoted in De Kruif, *Microbe Hunters*, p. 322.

29. Quoted in Gaynes, *Germ Theory*.

30. Quoted in bio., "Alexander Fleming," *Biography*, A&E Television Networks, 2014. www.biography.com.

31. Quoted in Gaynes, *Germ Theory*.

Chapter Four: Public Health

32. Quoted in Nancy Tomes, *The Gospel of Germs: Men, Women, and the Microbe in American Life*. Cambridge, MA: Harvard University Press, 1998, p. 7.

33. Quoted in Tomes, *The Gospel of Germs*, p. 124.

34. Quoted in Tomes, *The Gospel of Germs*, p. 121.

35. Quoted in Tomes, *The Gospel of Germs*, p. 98.

36. Quoted in Tomes, *The Gospel of Germs*, p. 127.

37. Gaynes, *Germ Theory*.

38. Quoted in Tomes, *The Gospel of Germ*, p. 135+.

39. De Kruif, *Microbe Hunters*, p. 300.

40. Centers for Disease Control and Prevention, "Achievements in Public Health, 1900–1999 Impact of Vaccines Universally Recommended for Children—United States, 1990–1998," *Morbidity and Mortality Weekly Report*, April 2, 1999. www.cdc.gov.

41. Donald G. McNeil Jr., "A Multitude of Vaccine Benefits, Yet Controversy Persists," *New York Times*, March 28, 2008. www.nytimes.com.

42. Gaynes, *Germ Theory*.

Chapter Five: The Unconquered

43. René Vallery-Radot, *The Life of Pasteur, Volume I*. New York: McClure, Phillips and Co., 1902, p. 281. http://books.google.com.

44. Miguel A. Faria Jr., "Medical History—Hygiene and Sanitation," *Medical Sentinel*, vol. 7, no. 4, Winter 2002. www.haciendapub.com.

45. Elizabeth Pfoh, Sydney Dy, and Cyrus Engineer, *Making Health Care Safer II: An Updated Critical Analysis of the Evidence for Patient*

Safety Practices, in *Evidence Reports/Technology Assessments,* no. 211, March 2013. Agency for Healthcare Research and Quality (US). www.ncbi.nlm.nih.gov.

46. Jonathan D. Katz, "Hand Washing and Hand Disinfection: More than Your Mother Taught You," Anesthesiology Clinics of North America, vol. 22, 2004, p. 466. www.handwashingforlife.com.

47. Gaynes, *Germ Theory.*

48. Barry Marshall, interview by Pamela Weintraub, "The Dr. Who Drank Infectious Broth, Gave Himself an Ulcer, and Solved a Medical Mystery," *Discover Magazine,* March, 2010. http://dis covermagazine.com.

49. Otula Owuor, "Ebola Outbreak: Why Africa Must Wake Up," *ScienceAfrica,* October 21, 2014. http://scienceafrica.co.ke.

50. Quoted in David Gorski, "Germ Theory Denialism: A Major Strain in 'Alt-Med' Thought," Science-Based Medicine, August 9, 2010. www.sciencebasedmedicine.org.

51. Philip S. Brachman, "Infectious Diseases—Past, Present, and Future," editorial, *International Journal of Epidemiology,* vol. 32, no. 5, 2003.

IMPORTANT PEOPLE IN THE HISTORY OF GERM THEORY

Emil von Behring: Working in Robert Koch's laboratory, von Behring was one of the pioneers of microbiology. He developed the first serum therapy for diphtheria, using the toxins that the diphtheria bacteria produce. Behring was renowned as "the savior of the children" for the thousands of children's lives saved with serum therapy and is also considered to be the father of the science of immunology.

Paul Ehrlich: Trained in Koch's laboratory, Ehrlich was an expert at staining and dyeing tissue samples and bacterial specimens, which led him to develop the theory of "magic bullets"— chemical compounds that targeted disease-causing bacteria while leaving all other tissues unharmed. He developed the first chemical treatment for a disease when he discovered a compound that kills syphilis microbes.

Alexander Fleming: Fleming discovered penicillin when a culture of staph bacteria was accidentally contaminated by the unusual mold that destroys bacteria. His curiosity about the substance and his belief that its actions were important revolutionized medicine and led the way to the modern development and use of antibiotics to cure infections.

Shibasaburo Kitasato: Trained in Koch's laboratory, Kitasato identified the bacterium that causes tetanus and isolated the toxin that the bacteria produce. He developed a serum therapy, or vaccine, based on the tetanus toxins to protect people against the disease. He also discovered the microbe that causes dysentery and independently isolated the bubonic plague bacterium at the same time that Alexandre Yersin did, although Yersin received the credit for the discovery.

Robert Koch: A founding father of germ theory and bacteriology, Koch developed the experimental method for proving that germs cause diseases and that a specific microbe causes a specific disease. Koch's postulates, the four criteria for demonstrating that a microbe causes a disease, are the basic principles still used today by scientists studying infectious diseases. Koch famously identified the bacterium responsible for tuberculosis in 1881.

Joseph Lister: Lister was one of the founders of germ theory. After reading Pasteur's descriptions of the diseases of fermentation, Lister applied the concept of germ theory to medical practice, specifically to surgery and wound treatment. He established antiseptic practices that successfully prevented many infections during wound treatment and surgical procedures and eventually convinced the medical establishment to adopt his methods. Lister is known as the "father of antiseptic surgery."

Louis Pasteur: The founding father of germ theory, Pasteur was a chemist and biologist renowned for his discoveries about the microbial world and his conceptualization of the germ theory of disease. He is also known for his development of vaccines, including the rabies vaccine, the process of pasteurization to eliminate microbial contamination, his proof that microbes do not spontaneously arise but "have parents," and his analysis of contagion and infection. Modern science credits Pasteur with being directly responsible for protecting millions of people from disease.

Walter Reed: Reed was a US Army physician who hypothesized and then proved that yellow fever is a mosquito-borne disease that could be prevented by avoiding mosquito bites and by controlling infected mosquitoes in the environment.

Pierre Paul Émile Roux: One of Pasteur's closest and most trusted colleagues, Roux assisted in the development of the rabies vaccine and in the discovery of the diphtheria bacterium and its toxin. Roux became the director of the Pasteur Institute in 1904, and he is also remembered for teaching the world's first microbiology courses.

Alexandre Yersin: At Pasteur's laboratories Yersin, along with Roux, isolated the toxin produced by the diphtheria bacterium and proved that the toxin caused the symptoms of the disease. He identified the bacterium responsible for bubonic plague during an outbreak in China. In later years he established a branch of the Pasteur Institute in Vietnam, where he resided for the rest of his life and worked on preparing serums and vaccines for plague and for cattle diseases.

FOR FURTHER RESEARCH

Books

Stephen Currie, *The Black Death*. San Diego: ReferencePoint, 2014.

Greenhaven Press (Editor), *Vaccines*. Farmington Hills, MI: Greenhaven Press, 2015.

Sheila Llanas, *Jonas Salk: Medical Innovator and Polio Vaccine Developer*. Edina, MN: ABDO, 2013.

Jim Murphy and Alison Blank, *Invincible Microbe: Tuberculosis and the Never-Ending Search for a Cure*. New York: Clarion, 2012.

Linda Wasmer Smith, *Louis Pasteur: Genius Disease Fighter*. Berkeley Heights, NJ: Enslow, 2015.

Tara C. Smith, *Ebola and Marburg Viruses*. New York: Chelsea House, 2010.

Christine Zuchora-Walske, *Antibiotics*. Edina, MN: ABDO, 2013.

Websites

Contagion: Historical Views of Diseases and Epidemics (http://ocp.hul.harvard.edu/contagion/index.html). At this extensive website from Harvard University, visitors can learn about some of the infectious diseases and epidemics that have occurred throughout human history. Included in the collection are articles written at the time of the epidemics, descriptions of many infectious diseases, and biographies of many important people who contributed to the germ theory of disease.

Institut Pasteur (www.pasteur.fr/en). The Institut Pasteur still exists today. Explore its website to learn about its mission and modern research efforts.

Lens on Leeuwenhoek (http://lensonleeuwenhoek.net). This site is dedicated to all things Leeuwenhoek, his works, his words, and his contributions to science.

Microbes (http://microbes.org). More than 10 million species of microbes live in the world. Learn about the habits, life cycles, benefits, and dangers of some of these microorganisms and explore the science of microbiology at this large website.

Robert Koch Institut (www.rki.de/EN/Home/homepage_node .html). The Robert Koch Institute in Berlin, Germany, has an English site where visitors can learn about its latest research into such varied topics as hygiene, diabetes, the Ebola virus, and the value of vaccines. Click on The Institute and History links to read about the scientific contributions of Robert Koch and the institution's origins.

Vaccines.gov (www.vaccines.gov). This website, from the federal government's Department of Health and Human Services, offers extensive information about the vaccines available today and their benefits, efficacy, and safety. Choose the Diseases link to read about specific diseases and the recommended vaccinations for them.

INDEX

PICTURE CREDITS